PRACTICAL FINANCIAL OPTIMIZATION
A Library of GAMS Models

PRACTICAL FINANCIAL OPTIMIZATION
A Library of GAMS Models

ANDREA CONSIGLIO
University of Palermo

SØREN S. NIELSEN†

STAVROS A. ZENIOS
University of Cyprus, and
The Wharton Financial Institutions Center

A John Wiley and Sons, Ltd., Publication

This edition first published 2009
© 2009 Stavros Zenios, Andrea Consiglio and Søren S. Nielsen†

Registered office
John Wiley & Sons Ltd, The Atrium, Southern Gate, Chichester, West Sussex, PO19 8SQ, United Kingdom

For details of our global editorial offices, for customer services and for information about how to apply for permission to reuse the copyright material in this book please see our website at www.wiley.com.

ISBN 978-1-4051-3371-5 (H/B)

A catalogue record for this book is available from the British Library.

Set in 11/13 Times by Laserwords Private Limited, Chennai, India
Printed in Great Britain by CPI Antony Rowe, Chippenham, Wiltshire

To Giusy and Camilla – A.C.
To Nina, Eleni and Andreas – S.A.Z.

Contents

Preface

Where the spirit does not work with the hand, there is no art.

Leonardo Da Vinci

This is a book about art: the art of modeling financial decision making using optimization. The science of financial optimization models has been introduced in the companion volume by S.A. Zenios, *Practical Financial Optimization: Decision Making for Financial Engineers* (Blackwell Publishing, Cambridge, MA, 2007), henceforth abbreviated as PFO.

In this book the reader's spirit works closely with his hand to create models. The reader is expected to have an understanding of creativity and to possess the skills and tools necessary to illustrate his or her ideas of business reality, finance concepts, and market expectations. The reader who has an unorthodox understanding of the problem is able to create a model that can act as a portal representing the realities of his or her own specific problem. This portal enables the user to perceive things from a decision maker's perspective, rather than from a broad and abstract perspective. In any event, the model does not teach a precise way of perception. The decision maker must maintain open-mindedness in order to question what has been created by the model, and how that interacts and relates with the decision making problem at hand. The decision maker comes to realize the great number of possibilities that are layered within any model.

Of course these possibilities must be well grounded in currently accepted theories of financial economics, while at the same time they should work well in practice and provide all the 'bells and whistles' required by the user. To paraphrase another Da Vinci quote, a good model must be a masterpiece of engineering and a work of art. But these issues were addressed in PFO. The current book leads the reader from the discussion of PFO to functional models implemented in the high-level algebraic modeling language GAMS – a *General Algebraic Modeling System* – of Brooke, Kendrick and Meeraus (1992). All models discussed in this book are available through the library FINLIB, which can be accessed from http://www.gams.com/finlib. The library provides instantiations of all the models discussed here, complete with market data. Users can readily substitute their own data in a model, or can use FINLIB to find the building blocks for their own models.

All the models in FINLIB can be run on any computer that supports GAMS and, therefore, are absolutely independent from the machine or the operating system. A student version of GAMS can also be downloaded free of charge from the web site. This version provides the full GAMS functionality, so that FINLIB models can be compiled by it. However, size restrictions apply to the number of variables and equations that can be solved. Therefore, large-scale instances of FINLIB models, with many asset classes, time-periods, scenarios, and so on, cannot be solved with the student version.

An explanation of the precise link between PFO, the current book, and FINLIB is in order. PFO introduces the general concepts and theories of financial optimization models that are used by financial engineers; it can be used as an introduction to the subject of financial modeling or as a stand-alone reference. The current book describes technical concepts relating to the implementation of GAMS models and discusses the implementation of several models from PFO, either verbatim or with small technical modifications. However, not all models in PFO are implemented here, although sufficient information is provided so that any additional models can be easily implemented by the reader. It is expected that this book will be used in conjunction with PFO, and references are made herein to PFO using the notation PFO-*m.n.p* where *m.n.p* refers to PFO labels. For instance, "Section PFO-6.3" refers to Section 3 of Chapter 6, and "Model PFO-6.4.2" refers to the second model of the fourth section of Chapter 6; readers will easily locate the cited material. Finally, FINLIB provides the software and the data required to instantiate all the models discussed in this book. There is a one-to-one correspondence between the models in the current book and FINLIB, and a strong relationship of all the models in FINLIB with PFO.

Organization of the Book

The organization of the chapters in this book closely follows the structure of PFO, with two introductory chapters, five chapters on optimization models and a chapter with several case studies.

The introductory part consists of Chapters 1 and 2, and gives an introduction to the GAMS modeling system and discusses data management. These chapters can be skipped by readers familiar with GAMS.

The bulk of the optimization models are given in the five chapters corresponding to the PFO chapters on portfolio optimization models; here we also develop one or more GAMS models for each model class. This part is the core of the book. It develops GAMS models for supporting the classic mean-variance analysis in Chapter 3, for fixed-income portfolios in Chapter 4, for scenario optimization in Chapter 5, for dynamic portfolio optimization using stochastic programming in Chapter 6, and for creating indexed portfolios in Chapter 7.

Finally, Chapter 8 deals with case studies and develops GAMS models for diverse real-world applications. The four sections in this chapter develop complete models for all the applications discussed in PFO: international asset allocation, corporate bond portfolio management, insurance policies with guarantees and personal financial planning. The models in this part capture policy restrictions, regulatory requirements, business objectives, and similar practical considerations, and they come complete with real-world data.

Acknowledgments

Some of the models developed in this book are based on our own published research, and we wish to express our appreciation to all colleagues and students from whom we have learned a great deal. Their contributions are gratefully acknowledged without implicating them in the final product.

Alex Meeraus, unquestionably the father of algebraic modeling languages and the founder of GAMS Development Corporation, has been not only a constant source of encouragement and a solid sounding board for ideas, but he also added a helping hand in compiling the library that accompanies this volume.

Over the years we have benefited from interaction with numerous collaborators. They all have had a significant impact on our work with financial modeling, and we thank them in strictly alphabetical order: Andrea Beltratti, Marida Bertocchi, Flavio Cocco, Rita D'Ecclesia, Rosella Giacometti, Ben Golub, Martin Holmer, Norbert Jobst, Roy Kouwenberg, Franz Nelissen, David Saunders, Nicholas Topaloglou, Hercules Vladimirou.

Sadly, during the writing of this book our colleague, student, and good friend Søren S. Nielsen passed away. His fingerprints are everywhere in this book, from the writing of the introduction to the GAMS modeling system, from the discussion of the models in several chapters, to the GAMS implementation of many models. The long delay in completing this volume is a sign of the great value that Søren added to the team, and his name features deservedly as a coauthor. But what was felt most was the absence of his great sense of humor during the long hours we toiled, occasionally together with Alex Meeraus, to complete this book and the accompanying FINLIB library.

This work was funded in part through European Commission contract ICA1-CT-2000-70015 establishing the *HERMES Center of Excellence on Computational Finance and Economics*, and also through research grants from the National Science Foundation (USA), Consiglio Nazionale delle Ricerche (Italy) and the Cyprus Research Promotion Foundation. Andrea Consiglio was partially supported by the research grant PRIN 2007TKLTSR.

Sincere appreciation is due to the Wiley editor Caitlin Cornish and assistant Aimee Dibbens who saw this project through with the utmost professionalism and good humor. Thanks for editing go to Kathy Stephanides; she did a superb job, thus allowing us to take the full credit for any remaining errors.

Palermo and Nicosia

Andrea Consiglio
consiglio@unipa.it
Stavros A. Zenios
zenios.stavros@ucy.ac.cy

Notation

We use throughout this book the notation introduced in S.A. Zenios, *Practical Financial Optimization: Decision Making for Financial Engineers*, (Blackwell Publishing, Cambridge, MA, 2007), abbreviated as PFO. To the extent possible the same notation is adopted in the accompanying software. Cross-references to chapters, sections, models, and so on from PFO are given using the notation PFO-*m.n.p* where *m.n.p* refers to PFO labels. For instance, "Section PFO-6.3" refers to Section 3 of Chapter 6, and "Model PFO-6.4.2" refers to the second model of the fourth section of Chapter 6. Readers will easily locate the cited material in PFO.

The current GAMS system, which includes the FINLIB, is available at: http://www.gams.com/download/.

The FINLIB is available at: http://www.gams.com/finlib/.

Sets and Indices

$U = \{1, 2, \ldots, n\}$ index set of available financial instruments or asset classes.

$\mathcal{T} = \{0, 1, \ldots, \tau, \ldots T\}$ set of time periods, from today (0) until maturity (T). Unless stated otherwise in the text all time periods are of equal duration, which is typically taken to be one month.

$\mathcal{K} = \{1, 2, \ldots, \kappa, \ldots, K\}$ index set of risk factors.

$\Sigma_t = \{1, 2, \ldots, S_t\}$ index set of states at period t.

$\Omega = \{1, 2, \ldots, N\}$ index set of scenarios.

i index of instrument or asset class from the set U.

t index of time periods from the set $\mathcal{T}$.

j index of risk factor from the set $\mathcal{K}$.

l index of scenario from the set Ω.

Variables and Parameters

x n-dimensional vector of investments in assets, with elements x_i. The units are in percentages of the total asset value or amounts in face value; the choice of units depends on the model and is made clear in the text.

b_0 n-dimensional vector of initial holdings in assets, with elements b_{0i}.

v_t^+ cash invested in short-term deposits at period t.

v_t^- cash borrowed at short-term rates at period t.

v_0 initial holdings in risk-free asset (cash).

p^l statistical probability assigned to scenario l.

$\tilde{r}$ n-dimensional random vector of asset returns, with elements $\tilde{r}_i$.

r^l n-dimensional vector of asset returns in scenario l, with elements r_i^l.

$\tilde{r}_t$ n-dimensional random vector of asset returns at period t, with elements $\tilde{r}_{ti}$.

r_t^l n-dimensional vector of asset returns at period t in scenario l, with elements r_{ti}^l.

r_{ft} spot rate of return of the risk-free asset at period t.

$\tilde{F}$ n-dimensional random vector of cashflows from assets, with elements $\tilde{F}_i$.

F^l n-dimensional vector of cashflows from assets in scenario l, with elements F_i^l.

$\tilde{F}_t$ n-dimensional random vector of cashflows at period t, with elements $\tilde{F}_{ti}$.

F_t^l n-dimensional vector of cashflows from the assets at period t in scenario l, with elements F_{ti}^l.

$\tilde{P}$ n-dimensional random vector of prices of assets, with elements $\tilde{P}_i$.

P^l n-dimensional vector of prices of assets in scenario l, with elements P_i^l.

$\tilde{P}_t$ n-dimensional random vector of prices at period t, with elements $\tilde{P}_{ti}$.

P_t^l n-dimensional vector of prices of assets at period t in scenario l, with elements P_{ti}^l.

$\tilde{P}_t^a$ n-dimensional random vector of ask prices at period t, with elements $\tilde{P}_{ti}^a$. In order to buy an instrument the buyer has to pay the price asked by traders.

$\tilde{P}_t^b$ n-dimensional random vector of bid prices at period t, with elements $\tilde{P}_{ti}^b$. In order to sell an instrument the owner must accept the price at which traders are bidding.

P_t^{al} n-dimensional vector of ask prices at period t in scenario l, with elements P_{ti}^{al}.

P_t^{bl} n-dimensional vector of bid prices at period t in scenario l, with elements P_{ti}^{bl}.

$\tilde{I}$ random variable of the total return of a benchmark portfolio or a market index.

I^l total return of a benchmark portfolio or a market index in scenario l.

$\tilde{L}_t$ random variable liability due at period t.

L_t^l value of the liability in scenario l.

Q a conformable covariance matrix.

$\sigma_{ii'}$ covariance of random variables indexed by i and i'.

$\rho_{ii'}$ correlation of random variables indexed by i and i'.

$\overline{x}_i$ maximum holdings in asset i.

$\underline{x}_i$ minimum holdings in asset i.

Glossary of Symbols

$\mathcal{E}[\tilde{r}]$ expectation of the random variable or vector $\tilde{r}$ with respect to the statistical probabilities p^l assigned to scenarios $l \in \Omega$.

$\mathcal{E}_{\mathcal{P}}[\tilde{r}]$ or $\mathcal{E}_{\lambda}[\tilde{r}]$ expectation of the random variable or vector $\tilde{r}$ with respect to the probability distribution $\mathcal{P}$ or the probabilities $\lambda \in \mathcal{P}$.

$\mathcal{U}(a)$ utility function with arguments over the real numbers a.

$\overline{r}$ mean value of a random variable or vector $\tilde{r}$.

$R(x; \tilde{r})$ portfolio return as a function of x with parameters $\tilde{r}$.

$V(x; \tilde{P})$ portfolio value as a function of x with parameters $\tilde{P}$.

$\max[a,b]$ the maximum of a and b.

Prob $(\tilde{r} = r)$ the probability that the random variable argument $\tilde{r}$ takes the certain value r.

I a conformable identity matrix.

1 conformable vector with all components equal to 1.

Abbreviations

ALM Asset and liability management.

APT Arbitrage Pricing Theory.

CAPM Capital Asset Pricing Model.

CBO Collateralized bond obligation.

CEexROE Certainty equivalent excess return on equity.

CEROE Certainty equivalent return on equity.

CLO Collateralized loan obligation.

CRO Chief risk officer.

CVaR Conditional Value-at-Risk.

EWRM Enterprise-wide risk management.

FHA Federal Housing Association.

LTCM Long Term Capital Management.

MAD Mean absolute deviation.

MBS Mortgage-backed security.

OAP Option adjusted premium.

OAS Option adjusted spread.

PFO *Practical Financial Optimization: Decision Making for Financial Engineers*, Blackwell Publishing, Cambridge, MA, 2007, by S.A. Zenios.

PSA Public Securities Association.

ROE Return on equity.

SPDA Single premium deferred annuities.

VaR Value-at-Risk.

GAMS General Algebraic Modeling System

IDE Integrated Development Environment.

List of Models

Chapter 1

An Introduction to the GAMS Modeling System

1.1 Preview

In this chapter we introduce the high-level algebraic modeling language that will be used in the rest of this book to build financial optimization models. The basic elements of the language are given first, together with details on getting started with the language, and the FINLIB library of models are also discussed here.

1.2 Basics of Modeling

Optimization is concerned with the representation and solution of models. Models can be represented in a number of ways, and they can be solved using a number of methods or algorithms. The General Algebraic Modeling System, GAMS, is a system for formulating and solving optimization models. It consists of a language that allows a high-level, algebraic representation of mathematical models, and provides a set of solvers, i.e., numerical algorithms, to solve them.

Why use algebraic modeling? Small models are easy to formulate and solve. They have a simple structure and one can simply edit a file containing the model's coefficients, and then call a standard linear programming solver to solve it. In fact, in the early days of optimization, models were solved using specialized *matrix generators* that provided the necessary input files for solvers. However, as models grow larger and become more complex, they become difficult to manage and to verify using this approach. GAMS was developed in response to the need for powerful and flexible front-end tools to manage large, real-life models. Large collections of data and models are only manageable when they possess structure, and algebra provides this structure in a well-known mathematical notation.

Conceptually, a model consists of two parts: The algebraic structure and the associated data instance. The formal linear programming model

$$\text{Minimize}_{x \in \mathbb{R}^n} \quad c^T x \tag{1.1}$$

$$\text{subject to} \quad Ax = b, \tag{1.2}$$

$$x \geq 0 \tag{1.3}$$

has the associated data *A, b, c*; see Appendix PFO-A for optimization basics. GAMS provides an algebraic framework for defining and manipulating data as well as building the models that use them. In addition to being concise and easily readable, the GAMS statement of a model is machine-independent and allows interaction with a number of solvers. Hence, it is not dependent on any particular optimizer or computer system.

The GAMS System consists of the GAMS compiler and a number of solvers. The compiler is responsible for user-interaction, by compiling and executing user commands given in a GAMS source file. A source file can implement a simple textbook problem, or it can represent a large-scale system consisting of several interrelated optimization models. The solvers are stand-alone programs that implement optimization algorithms for the different GAMS model types. The GAMS system can be called from the command line (for instance, a Unix prompt), or through the Integrated Development Environment (IDE), a windows-based environment that facilitates modeling by integrating editors with the GAMS system.

Section 1.3 gives an introduction to the GAMS language and Section 1.4 is a guide to quickly become accustomed to using GAMS. Readers who want a quick overview of GAMS modeling may start by reading Section 2.4, which contains a complete example drawn from financial planning.

1.3   The GAMS Language

Optimization models and their associated data are communicated to the GAMS system using a general-purpose language with elements of both ordinary programming languages (data declarations, control structures), and high-level modeling structures such as sets, equations, and models.

GAMS models are typically structured with the following building blocks:

1. *Sets*, which form the basis for indexation and serve as building blocks for data and model definitions.

2. *Data*, which are specified, either through direct statements (perhaps included in external files), or by calculating derived data.

3. *Variables and constraints*, which are used to define models, equations, and an objective.

4. An output section is sometimes used where the final results are calculated and presented.

In the remainder of this section we give an introduction to the elements of the language. In addition to the above-mentioned items, the main topics are *expressions*, which are used in assignment statements and in constraint declarations, and *control structures*, which lend programming language capabilities to GAMS. Readers who want to see a larger, complete modeling exercise may skip ahead to Section 2.4, and then refer back to this section for coverage of advanced features of the language when ready to embark on more substantial models.

1.3.1   Lexical conventions

A GAMS source file is an ordinary text file. The first character position on each line indicates how the line should be interpreted:

* (asterisk): A comment line, ignored by GAMS.

$ (dollar sign): Indicates a compiler directive or option. A list of the most common $-controls is given in Table 1.1. Many more exist than can be covered here; consult the User's Guide (see Notes and References at end of chapter) for complete information.

Any other character indicates a model source line. Customarily such lines start with a space character.

Table 1.1: The most common $-control commands. See Section 1.3.10 for examples of the use of $SET, $IF, $LABEL and $GOTO for conditional compilation.

Command	Description
$[ON|OFF]LISTING	Controls the echoing of input lines to the listing file
$[ON|OFF]SYMLIST	Controls the complete listing of all symbols
$[ON|OFF]TEXT	The $ONTEXT - $OFFTEXT pair encloses comment lines
$ABORT	This option will issue a compilation error and abort the compilation
$BATINCLUDE	The $BATINCLUDE option inserts a text file plus arguments used inside the include file
$CALL	Passes a followed string command to the current operating system command
$COMMENT	Changes the start-of-line comment symbol
$DOLLAR	Changes the current $ symbol
$ECHO	The echo option allows text to be written to a file
$EOLCOM	Redefines the end-of-line comment symbol
$GOTO	This option will cause GAMS to search for a line starting with $LABEL id
$IF	The $IF dollar control option provides control over conditional processing
$INCLUDE	The $INCLUDE option inserts a text file
$INLINECOM	Redefines the in-line comment symbols
$LABEL	This option marks a line to be jumped to by a $GOTO statement
$SET	Defines control variables
$STAR	This option is used to redefine the ****marker
$STITLE	This option sets the subtitle in the page header of the listing file
$TITLE	This option sets the title in the page header of the listing file

The main lexical elements of a GAMS statement are keywords, identifiers, and operators. The example model shows keywords in all capital letters, and identifiers use a mixture of upper and lower case, but the language is not case sensitive. Identifiers consist of letters, digits, or the underscore character, "_", and must begin with a letter (in early versions of GAMS, identifiers were limited to at most 10 characters).

The GAMS examples that follow use comments of the standard kind ("*" in position 1), but in addition assume that text that starts with the sequence "#" to the end of the current line is regarded as a comment. Hence, the command

```
$EOLCOM #
```

is assumed to be in effect in all examples. C++ and Java programmers might prefer to use the more familiar

```
$EOLCOM //
```

1.3.2   Sets

The primary tool for structuring large-scale models is the *set*. In any nontrivial model we will need to use data, variables, and constraints that are indexed, and sets form the basis for such indexing.

The simplest set declarations have the form:

```
SET Time                    /  2002 * 2006 /;   ALIAS (Time,t);
SET Bonds "Bonds universe" /GOVT_1 * GOVT_4/; ALIAS(Bonds,i,j);
```

These lines declare the two sets `Time` and `Bonds`. The set `Time` contains the elements from 2002 through 2006 (the asterisk indicates filling out the intervening elements; one could have written this: `SET Time /2002, 2003, 2004, 2005, 2006/;`). Similarly, the `Bonds` set contains bonds named `GOVT_1` through `GOVT_4`.

The ALIAS statement is a convenient way to declare indices to be used in connection with sets. The code above binds the name `t` to the set `Time`, and the names `i` and `j` to the set `Bonds`. These names can henceforth be used as indices into their associated sets (and only those sets).

The text "Bonds universe" in the `Bonds` declaration is an explanatory text that GAMS outputs in the listing whenever it lists the `Bonds` set, as a help in documentation. Such texts can occur in all declarations and can be a great help when reading GAMS listings. They need not be enclosed in quotation marks, but if they aren't then they cannot contain certain characters, which can lead to quite subtle syntax errors.

Indices and indexation

Most GAMS modeling elements (data, variables, etc.) can be indexed, with up to 10 indices. For instance, a two-dimensional parameter `F` can be defined over the sets declared above as (more on data declarations in Section 2.2.1):

```
PARAMETER F(Bonds, Time);  # -- or:
PARAMETER F(i, t);         # same thing
```

These two declarations have identical meaning, given the `ALIAS` declarations of `i` and `t`, and specify that `F` takes two indices belonging to (aliased to) the sets `Bonds` and `Time`, respectively.

Indices are used, for instance in expressions, to pick out individual elements of indexed objects. If `F(t,i)` is a bond's cashflows, then the following calculates each bond's total cashflows:

```
PARAMETER Total_CF(i);
Total_CF(i) = SUM(t, F(t,i));
```

and stores it into the declared one-dimensional parameter. Notice that this assignment is automatically performed for each value `i` in `Bonds`. There is more information on the summation operation in Section 1.3.3.

Leads and lags are indices that are shifted by some constant, as in `F(i,t+1)` or `F(i,t-1)`, respectively. The lead or lag need not be 1, but may be any integral expression whose value is known at compile time (endogenous). Leads and lags may only be used on static sets (not dynamic sets; see below).

There are no "index errors" in GAMS: If a lead or lagged index reaches beyond the underlying set, the result is 0; `F(i,t+1)` is 0 when `t` is the set's last element.

It is sometimes convenient to treat sets as being *circular*, so that leads beyond the end "wrap around" to the beginning and vice versa. This is indicated by using the ++ or \verb operator: `F(i++1,t)` references the next bond (from `i`), cyclically.

Constant set elements used as indices have to be specified in quotes:

```
F("GOVT_1", "2002") = 20000;
```

The ORD and CARD set functions

The `ORD` function takes as an argument the name of a set (or an index aliased to a set) and returns the ordinate value of the index relative to the set. The `CARD` function takes a set name (or index) and returns the cardinality of the set, i.e., the number of elements in the set:

```
P(i) $ (ORD(i) < CARD(i)) = 7;   # All elements except the last
                                 # set equal to 7
P(i) $ (ORD(i) = CARD(i)) = 3;   # and the last one set to 3
```

`ORD` is defined only on *static, one-dimensional* sets. They are not defined on constant set elements: `ORD("GOVT_4")` is illegal.

Subsets and multidimensional sets

A set can be declared as a subset of another set. For instance,

```
SET Callable(Bonds) /GOVT_1, GOVT_3/;
```

specifies a subset, `Callable`, of the `Bonds` set and declares bonds `GOVT_1` and `GOVT_3` as being callable bonds. Subsets can be multidimensional:

```
SET Matur(i,t)  / GOVT_1.2003, GOVT_2.2004,
                  GOVT_3.2005, GOVT_4.2006 /;
```

might specify the maturity years of the bonds as a subset of the cartesian product Bonds ×
Time. Note the dot-notation: GOVT_1.2003 specifies that the element (GOVT_1, 2003)
belongs to Matur.

Dynamic sets

The sets seen so far were all *static*. Their elements were explicitly listed as part of their
declaration. GAMS also allows *dynamic* sets, which are calculated during execution of
the model allowing them to change dynamically depending on some model characteristics. Dynamic sets are always subsets of another set (or other sets) and do not have the
/ ... / part in their declaration. Consider:

```
SET Time            /  2002 * 2006 /;   ALIAS (Time,t);
PARAMETER tau(t);
tau(t) = ORD(t) - 1;                 # Relative time:  0, 1, 2, ...


PARAMETER L(t), PV;

SET Sub(t); ALIAS (Sub, s);          # Dynamic subset of Time

Sub(t) = YES $ (tau(t) >= 1);        # All but the first year
L(t) $ (tau(t) < tau("2006")) = 7;#  # OK even with constant index
PV = SUM(s, tau(s) * L(s));          # OK even with dynamic set index
```

This fragment defines the set Sub as a dynamic subset of Time, and initializes it to contain
all but the first element. The expression YES $ (tau(t) >= 1) means to include element
t in Sub if the condition following the $-operator is satisfied (*conditional expressions* are
covered in detail in Section 1.3.3).

The ORD function is not defined on dynamic sets, but notice that a parameter such as
tau, which is declared on the static set Time, can be used with both constant arguments,
tau("2006") and with a dynamic set index, tau(Sub) or tau(s), as long as all arguments
belong to Time. This is a very useful technique to extend ORD-like mappings from dynamic,
even multi-dimensional, sets to numbers. CARD, however, is defined on dynamic (even
multidimensional) sets.

1.3.3   Expressions, functions, and operators

Data manipulations and constraint definitions require the use of *expressions* and *assignments*.
GAMS provides a rich set of operators and built-in functions for forming expressions.
Expressions are built up from numerical values, that is, *floating point constants, scalars,*
and *parameter* and *table* elements. Numerical values may be joined using *operators*; a list
of operators is given in Table 1.2. GAMS also defines a number of *functions*; see Table 1.3.
In addition, GAMS has a number of calendar (date/time) functions; see Table 1.4.

Table 1.2: Operators in GAMS expressions, grouped by priority. All operators accept and return numerical values. The logical operators interpret non-zero as true, and they return 0 or 1 for **false** or **true**.

Operator	Description
$	Conditional operator
**	Exponentiation
*,/	Multiplication and division
+,-	Addition and subtraction
LT, <	Less than
GT, >	Greater than
EQ, =	Equals
LE, < =	Less than or equal to
GE, > =	Greater than or equal to
NE, <>	Not equal to
NOT	Logical Not
AND	Logical And
OR	Logical Or
XOR	Logical Exclusive Or

Consider this simple example where some statistics of stock returns are calculated:

```
SET Time   /t1 * t5/;       ALIAS(Time, t);
SET Stock /stk1 * stk3/;  ALIAS(Stock, i, j);

TABLE Return(t, i) "Return of stock i in time period t,
   in percent"
            stk1     stk2     stk3
      t1      22       -8        4
      t2       3       20       12
      t3       3      -10        2
      t4     -30        8        1
      t5       3       -2        0 ;

PARAMETER MeanRet(i);  # Each stock's average return over time
MeanRet(i) = SUM(t, Return(t,i)) / CARD(t);

PARAMETER VarCov(i,j); # Variance-Covariance matrix of returns
VarCov(i,j) = SUM(t, (Return(t,i) - MeanRet(i)) *
                     (Return(t,j) - MeanRet(j))) / (CARD(t)-1);

DISPLAY MeanRet, VarCov;
```

Table 1.3: Functions in GAMS. Notes: (1) non-differentiable and results in discontinuous nonlinear programming model if used on (endogenous) variables; (2) not continuous and illegal when used on (endogenous) variables; (3) pseudo-random, may not occur in equation definitions; (4) takes one or more set indices as their first parameter and perform an indexed operation; (5) takes a set or index argument.

Function	Description	Note
ORD	Ordinate value of index	5
CARD	Cardinality of set	5
SUM	Summation over set	4
PROD	Product over set	4
SMIN	Minimum over set	4
SMAX	Maximum over set	4
ERRORF(X)	Integral of std. normal from $-\infty$ to x	1
EXP(X)	Exponential, e^x	
LOG(X)	Natural log (for $x > 0$)	
LOG10(X)	Base-10 log (for $x > 0$)	
NORMAL(X,Y)	Normal distribution; mean x, std.dev y	3
UNIFORM(X,Y)	Uniform distribution in $[x, y]$	3
ABS(X)	Absolute value	1
CEIL(X)	Smallest integer $\geq x$	2
FLOOR(X)	Largest integer $\leq x$	2
MAPVAL(X)	Mapping function (see User's Guide)	2
MAX(X,Y, ...)	Maximum of arguments	1
MIN(X,Y, ...)	Minimum of arguments	1
MOD(X,Y)	Remainder (modulo)	2
POWER(X,Y)	Power; y must be an integer	
ROUND(X)	Rounding to nearest integer	2
ROUND(X,Y)	Rounding to y decimal places	2
SIGN(X)	-1, 0 or 1 depending on the sign of x	2
SQR(X)	Square of x	
SQRT(X)	Square root	
TRUNC(X)	Rounding towards 0	2
ARCTAN(X)	Arcus tangent, result in radians	
COS(X)	Cos, x in radians	
SIN(X)	Sin, x in radians	

The first assignment statement assigns to `MeanRet(i)` the average return of the three stocks over the five time periods. GAMS automatically performs the assignment for each value of the index `i`; notice the use of the SUM function to perform the summation over the `t` index, and the use of the CARD function to average.

The $-operator and conditional expressions

The $-operator is somewhat unusual and deserves special attention. It is a binary operator, and the meaning of the expression `(exp) $ (cond)` is as follows.

Table 1.4: Date and Time functions in GAMS. Notes: (1) JDATE converts a date (given as year, month, day) into the day number, where "Day 1" is January 1, 1900; (2) JTIME converts a time (given as hour [0, ..., 23], minute [0, ..., 59], second [0, ..., 59]) into a fraction of a day; (3) these routines convert a day number into year, month, day, day of week, and check for leap years; (4) JSTART and JNOW return, in addition to date information, information on the time of day, taking no parameters; (5) these routines convert the result of JTIME, JSTART or JNOW back into time of day.

Function	Description	Note
JDATE(Y,M,D)	Day number	1
JTIME(H,M,S)	Time of day as fraction	2
GYEAR(J)	Year	3
GMONTH(J)	Month	3
GDAY(J)	Day of month	3
GDOW(J)	Day of week	3
GLEAP(J)	1 if leap year, 0 otherwise	3
JSTART	Start of current GAMS job	4
JNOW	Date and time when called	4
GHOUR(J)	Hour	5
GMINUTE(J)	Minute	5
GSECOND(J)	Second	5

```
(exp) $ (cond)       # GAMS conditional expression
(cond)? (exp) : 0    # Same construct in C/C++/Java
```

First, evaluate the expression cond. If its value is non-zero, then the complete expression has the value of exp, otherwise it has the value 0 and exp is not evaluated. For example, the annual cashflows of a set of bonds given their coupon rates and maturity years can be calculated by:

```
PARAMETER F(i,t);
 F(t,i) =        1       $ (tau(t)  = Maturity(i))
           + coupon(i) $ (tau(t) <= Maturity(i) and tau(t) > 0);
```

where tau(t) maps elements of the time set to calendar years; a bond's cashflow is composed of its price (negative at purchase), its principal payment (1, at maturity), and coupon payments; see Figures 2.1 and 2.2 for the complete model.

An expression such as tau(t) = 0 is called a *conditional expression*. GAMS has very simple rules for forming and using conditional expressions: any non-zero numerical value is interpreted as "true" when used in a conditional expression, and zero is interpreted as "false." Consistent with this, the relational operators (= , <, <= , >, >= , <>) and the logical operators AND, OR, and NOT return the numerical values 1 for "true" and 0 for "false." It is advisable to use parentheses around the operands of the $-operator; this aids readability and avoids any confusion about the priority of $ relative to other operators.

Notice also the use of an indexed set or parameter as a condition. Given the declarations

```
SET Matur(i,t);
PARAMETER F(t,i);
```

the expressions `Matur(i,t)` and `F(t,i)` are legal $-conditions, testing whether the pair `(i,t)` belongs to `Matur`, or whether `F(t,i)` is non-zero, respectively.

The $-operator also has another important function as a control structure: any time GAMS performs an indexed operation, a $-condition can be used to specify a subset of the indices over which the operation should be performed. Details are given in the relevant sections under equation definitions (Section 1.3.6), assignment statements (Section 1.3.4), and the SUM, PROD, SMIN and SMAX functions below.

Special functions: SUM, PROD, SMIN, SMAX

The functions SUM, PROD, SMAX, and SMIN have two arguments where the first must be a set (or index) expression. They form the sum, product, element-wise maximum, and element-wise minimum over the second argument values:

```
SUM(i, x(i));                 # sum of x's in a constraint
SMIN( (i,j), A(i,j));         # multidimensional indexation
```

Note the use of parentheses to sum over multiple indices.

The index set over which the operation is applied can be qualified using the $-operator, as in:

```
PROD(i $ Callable(i), x(i));   # conditional indexation
PROD(Callable(i), x(i));       # shorthand; same as above
```

```
* Find maximum below-diagonal element of A:
  SMAX( (i,j) $ (ORD(i) > ORD(j)), A(i,j));
```

The operation will be performed only over indices that satisfy the condition. When the condition is simply an indexed set or parameter, as in `Callable(i)`, the conditional summation can be abbreviated as shown in the second line above, which aids readability.

Applying one of these functions over an empty set results in the operations's *neutral element*: 0 for SUM, 1 for PROD, -INF for SMAX, and INF for SMIN. Comparing index values directly is not possible:

```
SMAX( (i,j) $ (i > j), A(i,j));         # Illegal!
SMAX( (i,j) $ (ORD(i) > ORD(j)), A(i,j)); # OK!

L(t) $ (t < "2006")         = 7;        # Illegal!
L(t) $ (tau(t) < tau("2006")) = 7;      # OK!
```

It is necessary to use some function that converts from set elements to numerical values, such as ORD or some parameter indexed by the set (as tau in the example above). For the special case of testing for equality, however, GAMS has a function SAMEAS:

```
SUM( (i,j) $ SAMEAS(i,j), A(i,j)); # Sum of A's diagonal elements
```

SAMEAS compares the names of the set elements referred to by the indices (not their ordinal values), and is legal even if the two indices belong to different sets.

Extended arithmetic: INF, EPS, NA, UNDF

GAMS defines certain special values that can be used in and result from expressions, but which are not numbers. The most common one is INF, which represents the (extended real) number ∞. For instance, a free VARIABLE has lower and upper bounds -INF and INF.

Another common special value is EPS, which is returned by solvers as the marginal value of degenerate variables or constraints (that is, non-basic variables or binding constraints with zero marginals). Knowing this makes it easy to pick out the final basis from a linear programming solution as those variables and (slack/artificial variables corresponding to) equations having "." as the marginal value as opposed to EPS or a non-zero value.

Finally, the last two special values are NA (used to represent missing, or "Not Available," data) and UNDF, for undefined (usually erroneous) results.

The rules for arithmetic using these values are well defined in GAMS but rather complicated; see the User's Guide or the library model crazy.gms for details.

1.3.4   Assignment statements

The assignment statement is used, as in any other language, to assign values to parameters (SCALARs, PARAMETERs, and TABLEs). The parameter on the left-hand side always has all indices specified, and GAMS automatically performs the assignment for each index value. Some examples:

```
left_over = 1-tax_rate;
Total_CF(i) = SUM(t, F(t,i));
P(i) $ (ORD(i) = CARD(i)) = 3;
```

The first line is a simple assignment of a single value. The second is performed for all indices i, the third only for those values of i that satisfy the condition. Note that in a conditional assignment that the condition is placed *before* the = sign.

Assignments performed over indices are performed in "parallel," in the sense that the right-hand side is first calculated for each index value, and only then is the left-hand side simultaneously updated. See in Section 1.3.9 (the LOOP statement) how this behavior can be circumvented if desired.

As a complete example, consider the following calculation of a lower-triangular matrix to hold covariance information:

```
SET Lower(i,j);
Lower(i,j) = YES $ (ORD(i) > ORD(j));

PARAMETER VarCov2(i,j);  # Lower-triangular Var-Covar matrix
VarCov2(i,i) = SUM(t, SQR(Return(t,i) - MeanRet(i))) / (CARD(t)-1);
```

```
VarCov2(Lower(i,j)) =
        2 * SUM(t, (Return(t,i) - MeanRet(i)) *
                    (Return(t,j) - MeanRet(j))) / (CARD(t)-1);
```

In this example we want to calculate variance-covariance information into a matrix efficiently, by only storing elements in the lower triangular half of the `VarCov2` matrix, defined by the dynamically calculated subset `SET Lower`. The assignment to `VarCov2(i,i)` calculates the diagonal, and the assignment to `VarCov2(Lower(i,j))` is shorthand for:

```
VarCov2(i,j) $ Lower(i,j) =  ...
```

so that only below-diagonal elements are assigned. Altogether, this calculation is almost twice as fast as calculating `VarCov` shown on page 7, yet used in a typical variance expression such as

$$
\text{SUM((i,j), x(i) * VarCov2(i,j) * x(j))}
$$

it is equivalent (but again about twice as fast to evaluate).

1.3.5   Variable declarations

Variable declarations are used to declare the variables used in a model. Variables can be *continuous* or *discrete* or some mixture of the two. Continuous variables are allowed to take on a range of variables between some (possibly infinite) lower and upper bounds, while discrete variables must take on an integer value between some finite bounds. The different declaration possibilities are shown in Table 1.5. Variables can have up to 10 indices.

Variable attributes

After declaration of a variable it is always possible to change its bounds:

```
POSITIVE VARIABLES y(i,j);
y.LO(i,j) = -4;
y.UP(i,j) = 10;
y.FX("2","3") = y.LO("2","3") + 18;
```

Table 1.5: The different kinds of variables and their declaration. The default bounds can be reset through the LO and UP (or FX) attributes.

Keyword	Type	Default Lower Bound	Default Upper Bound
FREE (Default)	Continuous	-INF	INF
POSITIVE	Continuous	0	INF
NEGATIVE	Continuous	-INF	0
BINARY	Discrete	0	1
INTEGER	Discrete	0	100

Here, a two-dimensional array of variables is declared as non-negative (default bounds 0 and ∞), but then the bounds are reset to -4 and 10, by setting LO and UP attributes. Finally, y("2","3") is *fixed* at a specific value. Assigning a value to the FX attribute is equivalent to setting the variable's lower and upper bounds to the same value. Fixing a variable does not remove it from the model; see the HOLDFIXED attribute on page 15 for how to do this. Variables also have two other attributes which are set by solvers: L is the "level" value (for instance the optimal value after the problem is solved), and M is the "marginal," or reduced cost. These can both be initialized by the user, which is useful in nonlinear programming to provide a starting point for the solver.

Variables also have a scaling attribute, SCALE; see the User's Guide for details.

1.3.6   Constraints: Equation declarations

Equations are used to declare and define model constraints:

```
EQUATIONS constr(i), objective;
constr(i) .. SUM(j, A(i,j) * x(j)) =L= b(i);
objective .. z =E= SUM(j, c(j) * x(j));
```

Here, we declare a set of constraints constr(i), and an individual constraint, objective. They are then defined (indicated by the ".." symbol). Each of the constraints constr(i) is a less-or-equal inequality constraint, as indicated by =L=. The objective constraint is an equality indicated by =E=. Greater-or-equal constraints are specified using =G=. A fourth relation, =N=, indicates that the constraint is present but non-binding; no use has yet been found for it. The expressions used to define constraints are covered in Section 1.3.3.

Endogenous variables in constraints

Constraint expressions are the only places where endogenous variables (GAMS variables), like x(j), can be used without their attributes (L, M, UP, LO, etc.). Note a few cautions regarding endogenous variables in constraints (an "endogenous expression" is an expression that is or contains an endogenous variable):

- nonlinear GAMS functions or operators, when used on endogenous expressions, lead to nonlinear (NLP or DNLP) models; see Section 1.3.8 for details on model types.

- non-continuous GAMS functions may not be used on endogenous expressions.

- the pseudo-random number generator functions UNIFORM and NORMAL may not be used at all in constraints.

- endogenous expressions cannot be used in the conditional part of a $-condition.

A $-condition may be placed before the .. symbol in a constraint definition. The constraint is only then generated and included in the model if the condition is satisfied:

```
constr(i) $ (ORD(i) > 3) .. SUM(j, A(i,j) * x(j)) =L= b(i);
objective $ 0 .. z =E= SUM(j, c(j) * x(j));  # constraint excluded
```

Equation attributes

Constraints have the attributes LO, UP, L and M. To understand these it is useful to consider, for instance, a less-equal constraint to be written as:

$$lhs = \text{L} = rhs$$

where *lhs* consists of all variable terms of the constraint and *rhs* consists of all constant terms. Then the level attribute .L is the value (after a solve) of the constraint's left-hand side, and the bounds attributes LO, UP are the bounds on it; for a less-equal constraint the left-hand side has bounds -INF and *rhs*. The M attribute is the constraint's dual price.

1.3.7   Model declarations

Model declarations serve to collect the constraints and variables that are part of the model, and to name the model.

```
MODEL Dedication /cfm, constr/;
```

Between the slashes are listed the names (without indices) of any constraints that should be part of the model Dedication. If all the constraints defined in the source file up to this point are part of the model, one can write:

```
MODEL Dedication /ALL/;
```

Model attributes

Models have "attributes" which are used to communicate information to and from a solver. Some are set by the user and correspond to setting the corresponding value using an OPTION statement; see Table 1.6. For instance, Dedication.RESLIM = 200; allows the solver to spend at most 200 seconds solving the Dedication model.

Others are set as a result of executing a SOLVE statement and they can be used to test the result of solving a model and hence decide on further actions to take:

Table 1.6: The most important OPTIONs. The argument N indicates a non-negative integer.

Keyword	Description
DECIMALS = N	Prints numerical values with N decimals
ITERLIM	Maximum number of solver iterations (default 1000)
LIMCOL = N	Lists N equations for each equation block (default 3)
LIMROW = N	Lists N variables for each variable block (default 3)
OPTCA, OPTCR	Sets optimality tolerance for MIP (see Page 15)
RESLIM	Maximum number of solver CPU seconds (default 1000)
SOLPRINT = ON/OFF	Lists the solution after each solve statement
SYSOUT = ON/OFF	Includes solver output files into listing

```
IF (Dedication.MODELSTAT = 1,   # Optimal! Solve another one:
   Solve Model2 MINIMIZING z USING lp;
ELSE
   DISPLAY "Could not solve Dedication";
 )
```

The most important values of MODELSTAT are 1: optimal, 2: locally optimal, 3: unbounded, and 4: infeasible;

Substituting fixed variables

The variable suffix FX will "fix" a variable, i.e., set its upper and lower bounds to the same value, but the variable is still present in the problem even though it has only a single feasible value. The MODEL attribute HOLDFIXED, when set to 1:

```
MODEL m /all/;
m.HOLDFIXED = 1;
```

will cause the values of all fixed variables to be substituted for the value throughout in the model. This can greatly reduce the complexity of a model, for instance converting a nonlinear model to a linear one. The only piece of information lost is the variable's dual information (marginal).

1.3.8   The SOLVE statement and model types

The SOLVE statement has the general form:

```
SOLVE model_name MINIMIZING obj_var USING model_type;
```

where model_name is the model to be solved, obj_var is the variable whose value should be minimized (one can also ask for MAXIMIZING the value), and model_type indicates the type of model to be solved; see Table 1.7. GAMS will select a default solver that is capable of solving the indicated model type, or a desired solver can be specified:

```
OPTION LP = BDMLP;
```

causes GAMS to use BDMLP to solve LP models.

The variable obj_var appearing in the SOLVE statement should be continuous without bounds.

Model types

GAMS recognizes several model types, as listed in Table 1.7. The most important are:

- LP: If the model contains only linear constraints and continuous variables, it's an LP. LP's are generally very easy to solve, except when extremely large.

- MIP: If the model contains linear constraints but discrete (integer or binary) variables, then it's a MIP model. These can be very time-consuming to solve. Be aware that

Table 1.7: GAMS Model types.

Keyword	Description	Variable and constraint typologies
LP	Linear Program	Linear
MIP	Mixed-integer Program	Linear, discrete
RMIP	Relaxed MIP	As MIP; solved as an LP
NLP	Nonlinear Program	Linear, nonlinear
DNLP	Discontinuous NLP	Linear, nonlinear, non-differentiable constraints
MINLP	Mixed-Integer NLP	Linear, discrete, nonlinear
RMINLP	Relaxed MINLP	As MINLP; solved as a NLP
MCP	Mixed Complementarity Program	Complementarity constraints
CNS	Constrained Nonlinear System	LP or NLP without objective function

INTEGER VARIABLES have implicit upper bounds of 100, so it is usually a good idea to set relevant upper bounds explicitly. Also, by default, a solution that is probably within 10 % of the optimum may be returned – to force the solver to go for an optimal one use OPTION OPTCR = 0. Also, the default iteration and resource limits of 1000 iterations and 1000 CPU seconds are, in some cases, not sufficient for the convergence of the solver. Use, for instance, OPTION ITERLIM = 999999999, RESLIM = 1200; to allow 20 minutes but virtually unlimited iterations for the solution.

- RMIP: To solve a MIP model while ignoring the integrality constraints, use RMIP. This is useful for model debugging.

- NLP: If your model contains nonlinear constraints and continuous variables, it's an NLP. These can be easy or difficult depending (mostly) upon whether the constraint set is convex, and the objective function convex (for minimization) or concave (for maximization). The best result possible for an NLP is "locally optimal"; the solver has no way to guarantee that a locally optimal solution is also globally optimal.

- MINLP: May contain nonlinear expressions and discrete variables.

- DNLP: May contain nonlinear constraints that are not differentiable, hence very unreliable to solve. One should usually try to reformulate such models, or "smooth" any "kinks."

1.3.9   Control structures

The control structures consist of the IF, WHILE, FOR, LOOP statements. They are used to control the execution of statements, depending on a condition. Control statements may not contain declarations.

The IF statement

The IF statement has the following forms:

```
IF (condition, stat-seq)
IF (condition, stat-seq ELSE stat-seq)
IF (condition, stat-seq ELSEIF condition, stat-seq ...
   ELSE stat-seq)
```

where condition is a conditional expression (1.3.3) and stat-seq is a semicolon-separated list of executable statements. Some examples follow:

```
IF (i < 0,
  DISPLAY "i is negative"
);

IF (i < 0,
  DISPLAY "i is negative"
ELSEIF i = 0,
  DISPLAY "i is zero"
ELSE
  DISPLAY "i is positive"
);
```

The IF ... ELSEIF ... variant allows an arbitrary number of ELSEIF parts, and the ELSE part is optional.

Iterative control structures

These statements allow repeated execution of groups of statements until some condition is satisfied (WHILE), or under control of either a scalar parameter (FOR) or a set index (LOOP). Their syntax is:

```
WHILE(condition, stat-seq)
FOR (parm = val1 TO/DOWNTO val2 BY val3, stat-seq)
LOOP(set-index, stat-seq)
```

where condition is a conditional expression (1.3.3) and stat-seq is a semicolon-separated list of executable statements. The FOR loop iterates a parameter parm through a range of values, as for instance:

```
PARAMETER p;
FOR (p = 10 TO 20 , stat-seq)      # p = 10, 11, 12, ..., 20
FOR (p = 20 DOWNTO 10 , stat-seq)  # p = 20, 19, 18, ..., 10
FOR (p = 0 TO 1 BY 0.1, stat-seq)  # p = 0, 0.1, 0.2, ..., 1
```

A powerful use of the iterative statements is to solve sequences of related models by having a SOLVE statement in the iteration. To use this facility it is necessary to know that every time a SOLVE statement is executed, the model is *regenerated* from scratch: GAMS runs through the equation definitions using the latest values of all sets and parameters they reference. By changing these as part of the iteration one can generate a different model in each run through the loop.

As an example, Figure 1.1 shows how to solve a sequence of related models under control of a FOR statement. The model is the Klee-Minty model (see, e.g., Nash and Sofer [1996] for a discussion on the Klee-Minty problem), which is interesting because it may require 2^m iterations with a naive implementation of the simplex algorithm, where m, the number of variables and constraints, is a parameter:

$$\underset{z \in \Re, x \in \Re^m}{\text{Maximize}} \quad z = \sum_{j=1}^{m} 10^{m-j} x_j \tag{1.4}$$

$$\text{subject to} \quad 2 \sum_{j=1}^{i-1} 10^{i-j} x_j + x_i \le 100^{i-1}, i = 1, \dots, m \tag{1.5}$$

$$x \ge 0 \tag{1.6}$$

As another example, Figure 1.2 shows the use of a LOOP to control the iterations, and a dynamic set s is used to control generation of the model. A solution report is built along the way.

```
SET base /1 * 10000/; ALIAS (base, j);    # Allow at most m = 10000
SET i(base);                              # A dynamic subset of base
PARAMETER numval(j);
numval(j) = ORD(j);            # Map set elements to numerical values

PARAMETER m;

EQUATIONS obj, constr(base);        # Declare constr over the base set

VARIABLE z; POSITIVE VARIABLES x(j);

obj        .. z =E= SUM(i, POWER(10, m-numval(i)) * x(i));
constr(i) .. 2 * SUM(j$(numval(j) < numval(i)),
                POWER(10, numval(i)-numval(j)) * x(j)) + x(i)
            =L= POWER(100, numval(i)-1);

MODEL KleeMinty /all/;

FOR (m = 1 TO 4,              # Solve a sequence of KleeMinty models
   i(j) = YES $ (numval(j) <= m);     # i contains  /1, 2, ..., m/;
   SOLVE KleeMinty MAXIMIZING z USING lp;
   DISPLAY m, z.L;
);
```

Figure 1.1: GAMS model for solving the Klee-Minty problem for $m = 1, 2, 3, 4$.

```
SET control /1*1000/; ALIAS(control,c);
SET s(control);                               # a dynamic subset
* Tiny model to be solved:
VARIABLE x, z;
EQUATION eqn;
PARAMETER parm(c) /1 = 10, 2 = 50, 3 = 80/; # some data

eqn(s) .. z = E = SQR(x) + parm(s); # depends on contents of s
x.LO = 0.1; x.UP = 100;

MODEL testmodel /all/;

PARAMETER solution(control, *);
PARAMETER converged; converged = 0;

LOOP(c $ (NOT converged),        # c is used only within the loop
   s(control) = YES $ (ORD(control) = ORD(c)); # controls eqn(s)

   SOLVE testmodel MAXIMIZING z USING NLP;

   solution(c, "parm") = parm(c);
   solution(c, "x") = x.L;
   solution(c, "obj") = z.L;
   converged = ...;  # 1 when converged and want to terminate
);
DISPLAY solution;
```

Figure 1.2: Using a LOOP iterative statement to control a SOLVE statement and to create an iteration-by-iteration solution report. Notice the way the three sets/indices (control, s, and c) are declared and used: control is the base set, allowing up to 1000 iterations; c is the loop control index; and s is a dynamic subset of the control set, which (in this example) contains the the current loop index as its only element, and which in turn controls the generation of equation eqn. The loop can be terminated at any time by setting converged to 1.

Defeating parallel assignment

An assignment statement such as

```
MeanRet(i) = SUM(t, Return(t,i)) / CARD(t);
```

is executed "in parallel": GAMS performs the assignment for each value of the controlling index i "at once." But sometimes the parallel assignment feature gets in the way. Consider calculating the Fibonacci numbers from 1 to 100. One might be tempted to do this:

```
SET i /1*100/; ALIAS(i,j);
PARAMETER Fibonacci(i);
```

```
Fibonacci ("1") = 1;
Fibonacci ("2") = 2;
Fibonacci (i) = Fibonacci (i-1) + Fibonacci (i-2); # Bad idea!
```

The last assignment would not work because of the "parallel assignment" feature of GAMS: Most of the values referenced on the right-hand side are equal to zero (i.e., Fibonacci ("3") through Fibonacci ("100")), and the values assigned to Fibonacci ("1") through Fibonacci ("2") use undefined indices, -1 and 0. The way to implement this kind of *recurrence relation* is to force GAMS to execute the assignment element-by-element in a specified order, rather than in parallel. The LOOP statement does this:

```
Fibonacci ("1") = 1;
Fibonacci ("2") = 2;
LOOP (i $ (ORD (i) > 2),
   Fibonacci (i) = Fibonacci (i-1) + Fibonacci (i-2); # OK!
);
```

Note the use of the $-operator to limit the LOOP statement to values of i greater than 2.

1.3.10   Conditional compilation

Some of the GAMS $-control commands (see Table 1.1) are particularly useful for conditional compilation, that is, including or excluding parts of the GAMS source code depending on some condition. We give here an example:

```
$SET switch 2          # Select this case among several

 DISPLAY "beginning...";

$IF NOT "%switch%" == "1" $GOTO case2
    DISPLAY "case 1";
$   GOTO continue

$LABEL case2
$IF NOT "%switch%" == "2" $GOTO case3
    DISPLAY "case 2";
$   GOTO continue

$LABEL case3
$IF NOT "%switch%" == "3" $GOTO error
    DISPLAY "case 3";
$   GOTO continue

$LABEL error
    ABORT "switch has an illegal value";

$LABEL continue
    DISPLAY "Carrying on...";
```

1.4   Getting Started

The GAMS system can be executed in two modes. On computers running Windows, through an Integrated Development Environment graphical interface that facilitates managing the files involved in a GAMS project. On computers running Unix, through a simpler command-line interface where the GAMS system is called from a command-line window. Both modes of execution are described below.

1.4.1   The Integrated Development Environment

The GAMS Integrated Development Environment (IDE) provides an environment for managing GAMS modeling projects that facilitates the process of editing input files, executing GAMS, and viewing output files. It is a graphical environment that is available on Windows systems, and is expected to be available on Unix systems as well.

The GAMS IDE is project-oriented. This means that all the files associated with a model, or a set of models, are collected in a *project file*. Even if your GAMS "project" consists of only a single GAMS input file and its output file, there are advantages to organizing these files in a project.

Creating a new GAMS project

To create a new GAMS project, first close any open files in the GAMS IDE ("File – Close" for each one). Then open the "File – Project – New Project" window and navigate to the directory where you want your project to reside (you may already have your GAMS source file there). Under "File name," enter the name of your project. To add existing source files to your project, use "File – Open" and navigate to your source files (usually .gms and .inc files), adding them to the project one by one (or add multiple files at once, using the standard key sequences). To create a new source file in your project, use "File – New"; then immediately after "File – Save as" to give the new file a name.

Opening an existing GAMS project

Use "File – Project", to check if the project is already listed in the window, or click "Open project" and navigate to it.

Executing GAMS models

To execute a GAMS source (.gms) file, make sure it is the active file in the IDE ("has focus"). Then use the Run entry from the File menu, press F9 or click on the Run icon at the top of the main window. Next to the Run icon is an entry field to specify additional parameters for the GAMS run. Additional parameters have the same effect as if they were specified from the commandline.

While GAMS is compiling and executing the model it displays a log window showing what is going on. If the run takes a while, you may check the Update entry at the bottom to make sure the log window is updated every time GAMS or one of the solvers outputs a line. After execution, the listing file is made the active file, and can be examined for the solution or any error messages.

1.4.2   Command line interaction

The simplest and most general way to use the GAMS system is from the command line through text files. An input file containing the model's source code, and having a name with the extension .gms, is created using an ordinary text editor, such as vi, emacs, or Notepad (if using a word processor you should "save as type .TXT"). This file is then submitted to the GAMS system by issuing the command:

```
gams dedicate
```

from the Unix prompt. GAMS will look for and compile the file dedicate.gms, and generate an output file, dedicate.lst, containing a listing of the input file and the solutions of any models solved. This file is then examined using a text editor. It is often convenient to have several open windows: one in which to edit the input file, one to call GAMS, and one to look at the output.

1.4.3   The model library

The fastest way to build a new model, or to learn the language, is to study existing models that address a related problem. The GAMS system includes a large library of models that demonstrate applications drawn from engineering, finance, and economics. The library is an excellent resource for learning GAMS, or for learning about modeling in a particular problem area. The FINLIB library, which is documented in this book, contains several of the financial optimization models discussed in the companion volume *Practical Financial Optimization*.

From the GAMS IDE, "File – Model Library – Open GAMS Model Library" gives access to more than 100 models in the standard library and to the FINLIB library. Clicking on one of the models will add it to your current project and you can now modify it as you want (you will not be allowed to modify the original file).

From the command line,

```
gamslib index
```

copies a file containing a list of the library models into the current directory; the commands

```
gamslib 1
gamslib dedicate
```

both copy model number 1, dedicate.gms, into the current directory.

Notes and References

The GAMS manual, *GAMS: A User's Guide* and other documents can be downloaded from http://www.gams.com. A demonstration version of the GAMS system can be obtained from http://www.gams.com/download.

At the time of writing it is also possible to download the GAMS Integrated Developer Environment (for Windows), containing a sample of solvers and the GAMS main compiler. This system runs in "demo mode," allowing the solution of small to medium-sized models. To obtain licenses for solving larger models, for other solvers, or for systems for other machines, contact support@gams.com.

Chapter 2

Data Management

2.1 Preview

In this chapter we discuss issues relating to the management of data in GAMS models. Together with the previous chapter we complete here the introduction to GAMS, and in Section 2.4 a complete example drawn from financial planning, namely portfolio dedication, is presented.

2.2 Basics of Data Handling

It is unclear whether the heart of a financial optimization model for decision making is the data or the mathematical model. Both are indispensable for a functional and effective system: functional in that it works, and effective in that it solves the real-world problem it was designed to solve in the first place.

It is not uncommon in financial decision making for the user to deal with hundreds or even thousands of financial assets, in a variety of currencies and markets, extending over long time horizons that may run several decades into the future. Furthermore, uncertainty is prevalent and may need hundreds or thousands of scenarios to be dealt with. The user most likely will require that very large sets of data be manipulated and input to a mathematical model in order to instantiate (i.e., create a single instance of) the model that reflects the specifics of his or her problem. Hence, data handling is a critical step in all modeling applications and financial decision making is no exception.

One very important principle concerning the use of data when building models is that:

Data should be entered in its most basic form, and each data item should be entered only once.

In this way we avoid two potential pitfalls. First, entering data in its most basic form allows us to change them easily and safely, and all derived data are updated automatically. For instance, it is better to input spot rates and then use GAMS to calculate forward rates, than to input both spot and forward rates. It is better, too, to input a time series of prices and then calculate returns, than to input both prices and returns. If a price changes the GAMS code will recalculate returns, thus avoiding potential errors of data inconsistency. Second, we can isolate the input data from the algebraic representation of the model, which makes the model easier to read by other users and to be adapted to new data sets. It is good practice to keep all data separately at the beginning of a model, usually as an external input file, rather than to intersperse data with the model, and input them just before they are needed.

GAMS statements offer several formats for data as one-dimensional lists, two-dimensional tables and even multi-dimensional data structures. GAMS also offers several features to input external files so that data are kept separate from the model. Furthermore, data can be read in different formats, thus making GAMS compatible with the files generated by database management systems, spreadsheets, or other software for generating financial data. Similarly, GAMS offers features for data output and report preparation. All these features are explained next.

2.2.1   Data entry: SCALARS, PARAMETERS, and TABLES

Numerical data in GAMS are entered as SCALAR, PARAMETER, or TABLE:

SCALAR: a single real number (no indices allowed)

PARAMETER: an indexed data collection (1–10 indices) of numbers

TABLE: a syntactically convenient way to declare and initialize a parameter.

All GAMS data are of double-precision, floating-point type. SCALAR, PARAMETER, and TABLE declarations differ in their initialization syntax as described in the examples below.

SCALARS

```
SCALAR tax_rate /0.50/;
SCALAR left_over;

left_over = 1-tax_rate;

DISPLAY "New tax rate: ", tax_rate;
```

This example shows the declaration and immediate initialization of a SCALAR, tax_rate, and the declaration of another scalar, left_over, which is not immediately initialized. Initialization can occur in a later assignment statement, as shown. Scalars (or parameters) may not be used before they are initialized. The output statement (DISPLAY) is explained in Section 2.2.3.

PARAMETERS

PARAMETERS are data sets indexed by one or more indices. Indices are sets (or set aliases) that are previously declared (and initialized, if the parameter is initialized). In the following example two parameters are declared: one initialized as part of the declaration, the other left un-initialized at first, then later initialized by assignment:

```
PARAMETER discount(t)
        / 2002 = 0.9, 2003 = 0.85, 2004 = 0.80,
          2005 = 0.75, 2006 = 0.70                    /;
```

```
PARAMETER tau(t) "relative time corresponding to t, in years"
          / 2002 = 1, 2003 = 2, 2004 = 3, 2005 = 4, 2006 = 5 /;

PARAMETER yield(t);
yield(t) = -LOG(discount(t))/tau(t);

DISPLAY discount, yield;
```

An example of the declaration and initialization of a three-dimensional parameter follows:

```
PARAMETER Correlation(i,j,t) /
    GOVT_1.GOVT_2.2002                                    = 0.2,
    (GOVT_2*GOVT_4).(GOVT_1*GOVT_4).(2003*2006) = 0.3 /;
```

The construct on the right means that `Correlation(i,j,t)` is initialized to 0.2 for bonds `GOVT_1` and `GOVT_2` in 2002 and to 0.3 for the 48 combinations of indices indicated.

TABLES

A TABLE declaration is just a syntactically convenient way to declare a multidimensional parameter. For instance, a two-dimensional parameter can be declared and initialized as a table:

```
TABLE CashFlow(t,i)
                  GOVT_1      GOVT_2      GOVT_3      GOVT_4
       2002        0.05        0.05        0.05        1.05
       2003        0.06        0.06        1.06
       2004                    1.00
       2005        1.04                                        ;
```

The elements specified in a table must be positioned on the same row and column as the corresponding indices. Omitted entries correspond to zeroes. This example specifies, for instance, that

```
CashFlow("2003","GOVT_2") = 0.06
```

and

```
CashFlow("2004","GOVT_1") = 0.
```

All of the `CashFlow` entries for 2006 are 0. The elements specified must be numerical constants and cannot be expressions.

To declare parameters with three or more indices in a tabular format, use the "dot"-notation:

```
TABLE VarCov(i,j,t)    "Time-dependent Variance-Covariance Data"
                       2002   2003   2004   2005   1999
       GOVT_1.GOVT_2    0.3    0.4    0.3    0.2   -0.2
       GOVT_2.GOVT_2           0.3    0.4
```

```
      GOVT_2.GOVT_3        0.3    0.4
      GOVT_2.GOVT_4                              -0.2;
```

Tables with three or more dimensions can have set elements corresponding to any number of indices specified vertically (down along the first column) or horizontally (along the top line), separated by periods. The set elements specified must belong to the index sets, for instance, "GOVT_1", "GOVT_2", "2002" correspond to sets indexed by i, j, t, respectively.

Large tables can be split using a plus sign:

```
  TABLE VarCov(i,j,t)   "Time-dependent Variance-Covariance Data"
      GOVT_2.2002 GOVT_2.2003 GOVT_2.2004 GOVT_2.2005 GOVT_2.2006
  GOVT_1    0.3        0.4         0.3         0.2         -0.2
  GOVT_2               0.3         0.4


      + GOVT_3.2002    GOVT_3.2003   GOVT_4.2004
  GOVT_2      0.3          0.4          -0.2      ;
```

In addition to specifying data directly in the source file, GAMS also interacts with databases and spreadsheets; see the GAMS User's Guide for further information.

Exogenous versus endogenous variables

Terms such as variable or parameter mean slightly different things in different contexts. In optimization, a variable represents a decision to be made.

When GAMS solves an optimization model, the solver finds appropriate values for the variables that satisfy the model's constraints. In economic literature such variables are sometimes called *endogenous* variables, in contrast to *exogenous* variables, or *parameters*. GAMS parameters may be assigned and modified as part of the model setup, and therefore act somewhat like ordinary programming language variables, but once the model is being solved they are fixed for the duration of the SOLVE statement. In summary, GAMS VARIABLES are *endogenous variables*; SCALARs, PARAMETERs, and TABLEs are *exogenous variables*.

2.2.2   External data files: INCLUDE

It is good practice to gather all the data statements of a model in a separate file. This file can be created using sophisticated data management systems, such as a relational database or a spreadsheet, and then can be included in the source file of the GAMS model. In this way not only are the data kept separately from the model, but the management of files is also eased and errors avoided.

Assuming that all data are gathered together in file ModelData.inc, then the code segment

```
$INCLUDE ModelData.inc;
```

will include the data in the source file of the GAMS model.

We use the .inc extension when the file contains GAMS data structures, i.e., it includes scalars, parameters, and tables that have been properly defined in GAMS. However, it is also possible to communicate with files created with Excel or with plain text files.

GAMS communicates with Excel via GDX (GAMS Data Exchange) files. A GDX file is a file that stores the values of one or more GAMS symbols such as sets, parameters, variables, and equations. GDX files can be used to prepare data for a GAMS model, present results of a GAMS model, store results of the same model using different parameters, etc. A GDX file does not store a model formulation or executable statements. GDX files are portable between different platforms. In order to write data from GAMS to Excel, the user writes a GDX file and then reads the Excel file from the GDX file: GAMS → GDX → Excel. This is practically seamless for the user and requires few commands as discussed in the GAMS Users's Guide. The process for importing data from an Excel file to GAMS is similar: Excel → GDX → GAMS.

Plain text files can be imported with the CSV format; CSV stands for comma-separated values, sometimes also called comma delimited. A CSV file is a specially formatted plain text file that stores spreadsheet or basic database-style information in a very simple format, with one record on each line, and each field within that record separated by a comma. It is of course important that the individual "records" within a CSV file do not contain commas, as this may break the simple formatting when using the file in another application.

CSV files are often used as a simple way to transfer a large volume of spreadsheet or database information between programs, without worrying about special file types. For example, scenario generators could be written in C, C++, Matlab, or other simulator software. It is convenient to print the results in an ASCII file and separate the records by commas. Then, using the GAMS dollar statements ONDELIM and OFFDELIM, the data can be read in the GAMS model file.

2.2.3   Output: DISPLAY and PUT

The easiest way to output data and results is the DISPLAY statement:

```
DISPLAY VarCov, discount, tau;
DISPLAY X.L, X.LO, X.UP, X.M, EQN.M;
```

Scalar and parameter data are specified without indices (i.e., VarCov, not VarCov(i,j,t)). To display variables and equations, such as X or EQN, it is necessary to specify which attribute we wish to display: X.L is the level values, X.M the marginal values, and X.UP, X.LO the bounds.

The OPTION statement provides some control over the output format. OPTION DECIMALS = 8 causes data to be displayed with 8 decimals, and OPTION X:8 does the same for data related to the symbol X.

Multidimensional data are displayed in a tabular format. The option Matrix:d:r:c causes GAMS to display using d decimals, listing the last c indices across the top, the next r indices in the left-most column, and any remaining indices in separate tables. For instance, a simple DISPLAY VarCov results in:

```
----    PARAMETER VARCOV   Time-dependent Variance-Covariance Data

                     2002     2003     2004     2005     2006

GOVT_1.GOVT_2     0.300    0.400    0.300    0.200   -0.200
GOVT_2.GOVT_2              0.300    0.400
```

```
GOVT_2.GOVT_3     0.300     0.400
GOVT_2.GOVT_4                          -0.200
```

whereas a DISPLAY VarCov:1:1:1 results in:

```
----   PARAMETER VARCOV   Time-dependent Variance-Covariance Data
INDEX 1 = GOVT_1
                  2002     2003     2004     2005     2006

  GOVT_2          0.3      0.4      0.3      0.2     -0.2

  INDEX 1 = GOVT_2

                  2002     2003     2004

  GOVT_2                   0.3      0.4
  GOVT_3          0.3      0.4
  GOVT_4                  -0.2
```

using a separate table for each value of the first index.

The PUT statement

To get complete control over output formats and to print to files (other than the listing file), the PUT statement is used. A simple example follows:

```
SET i /i1*i10/;
PARAMETER P(i);
p(i) = 2*SIN(ORD(i));

FILE out /output.dat/;     # Declare the output file and name it
PUT  out;                  # Make 'out' the active output file

# Print various things
PUT 'Here is my output:' / / /;
PUT #1@40 'Here is line 1, column 40' /
LOOP(i,
   PUT 'Element ', ORD(i):2:0, ' of p = ', p(i) / ;
);

PUTCLOSE out;              # close the output file
```

The / character in a PUT statement causes a line break; the notation #1@40 places any following output at line 1, column 40. The formatting characters in ORD(i):2:0 specify 2 positions and no decimals.

2.3   Data Generation

We have not touched upon the issue of data generation. This of course is not a problem for GAMS, and it is the user's responsibility to generate the data that apply to the problem at hand. It is fair to assume that a user has a good understanding of the data of his or her problem before the issue of optimal decision making becomes relevant. After all, the financial optimization models aim at improving the decision making process, and whatever process was used in the past must have relied on problem data. There is a vast finance literature on pricing, forecasting, and econometric modeling, and it provides the data required for optimization studies.

The large majority of the optimization models we implement are scenario-based, and methods for scenario generation are discussed in Chapter PFO-9. Specific examples are given in the various application sections both in PFO and later in this book.

2.4   A Complete Example: Portfolio Dedication

We now describe in detail a small, but complete, GAMS model that solves the portfolio dedication Model PFO-4.2.3. The material in this section will enable the reader to understand most of the models in this book. Additional features of the language are needed to implement the more complicated case studies, but the material in the simple example presented here provides the foundation on which the more advanced models are built.

The portfolio dedication model we use is a version of the PFO model. The differences in the model implemented here compared to the model given in PFO is that the bond price P_i is included explicitly at time 0 instead of being part of the cashflow parameter F_{0i}, and borrowing is not allowed ($v_t^- = 0$). The formal model is given as follows:

Model PFO-4.2.3 Portfolio dedication

$$\text{Minimize } v_0 \tag{2.1}$$

$$\text{subject to} \qquad v_0 - \sum_{i=1}^{n} P_i x_i = v_0^+, \tag{2.2}$$

$$\sum_{i=1}^{n} F_{ti} x_i + (1 + r_{f(t-1)}) v_{t-1}^+ = L_t + v_t^+,$$

$$\text{for all } t \in \mathcal{T}, \tag{2.3}$$

$$x, v^+ \geq 0. \tag{2.4}$$

Recall that the problem is to purchase a bond portfolio whose proceeds (coupon and principal payments) are sufficient to cover liabilities in each of a series of future time periods. Surplus cash in each period can be reinvested to the next, v_t^+. The optimal portfolio is the one that requires the smallest initial outlay v_0 to purchase; this outlay is equal to the portfolio price (given by $\sum_{i \in U} P_i x_i$) plus the initial reinvestment.

2.4.1   The source file

The GAMS implementation of the model `DedicationNoBorrow.gms` is found in
Figures 2.1 and 2.2. See Section 1.3.1 for an overview of GAMS lexical conventions.

```
SET Time Time periods /2001 * 2011/;

ALIAS (Time, t, t1, t2);

SCALARS
   Now       Current year
   Horizon   End of the Horizon;

   Now = 2001;
   Horizon = CARD(t)-1;

PARAMETER
   tau(t) Time in years;

* Note: time starts from 0

   tau(t)   = ORD(t)-1;

SET Bonds Bonds universe
     /DS-8-06, DS-8-03, DS-7-07,
      DS-7-04, DS-6-11, DS-6-09,
      DS-6-02, DS-5-05, DS-5-03, DS-4-02
      /;

ALIAS(Bonds, i);

PARAMETERS
        Price(i)        Bond prices
        Coupon(i)       Coupons
        Maturity(i)     Maturities
        Liability(t)    Stream of liabilities
        rf(t)           Reinvestment rates
        F(t, i)         Cashflows;

* Bond data. Prices, coupons and maturities from the Danish market

$INCLUDE "BondData.inc"
```

Figure 2.1: GAMS representation of the portfolio dedication model `DedicationNoBor-row.gms`. Data and parameter settings.

```
Price(i)      = BondData(i,"Price")/100;
Coupon(i)     = BondData(i,"Coupon")/100;
Maturity(i) = BondData(i,"Maturity") - Now;


F(t,i) = 1$(tau(t) = Maturity(i))
          + coupon(i) $ (tau(t) <= Maturity(i) and tau(t) > 0);

PARAMETER
     Liability(t) Liabilities
     /2002 =   80000, 2003 = 100000, 2004 = 110000, 2005 = 120000,
      2006 = 140000, 2007 = 120000, 2008 =   90000, 2009 =   50000,
      2010 =   75000, 2011 = 150000/;


DISPLAY BondData,Liability;
```

Figure 2.1: Continued

```
POSITIVE VARIABLES
     x(i)             Face value purchased
     surplus(t)       Amount of money reinvested;

VARIABLE
     v0               Upfront investment;

EQUATION
  CashFlowCon(t) Equations defining the cashflow balance;

CashFlowCon(t)..
     (SUM(i, F(t,i) * x(i))) +
     (v0 - SUM(i, Price(i) * x(i)))      $(tau(t) = 0) +
     (( 1 + rf(t-1) ) * surplus(t-1))    $(tau(t) > 0) =E=
      surplus(t) + Liability(t)          $(tau(t) > 0);

MODEL Dedication /CashFlowCon/;

SOLVE Dedication MINIMIZING v0 using LP;

DISPLAY v0.L,x.L,surplus.L;
```

Figure 2.2: GAMS representation of the portfolio dedication model `DedicationNoBor-row.gms`. Variables and equations.

Sets and data

The structure of the GAMS model follows the formal model closely. First, we use `Time` to denote the set $T = \{1, 2, \ldots, T\}$. This instance of the model covers the years 2001 through 2011, indicated by the notation `/2001 * 2011/`. The `ALIAS` statement indicates that we intend to use the index `t` to index the set `Time`. The next few lines introduce auxiliary data: the `SCALAR` `Now` that defines the starting point of the planning horizon, and a `PARAMETER` `tau(t)` that defines a mapping from the elements of the set `Time` into the real numbers, starting from 0. By convention, the term scalar is used for single numbers, whereas parameter usually is for vectors having one index. Multi-dimensional data can be specified as either parameters or as tables; see below.

The actual values of the parameter `tau` are calculated in the assignment statement `tau(t) = ORD(t) - 1`; the `ORD` function maps the index `t` to its ordinal value in the set `Time`, so that `ORD("2001") = 1`, etc. Even when set elements appear as numbers, GAMS does not by itself associate numerical values to them (except through the `ORD` function). Hence, the `tau` parameter is needed to associate the year 2001 with the numerical value 0 (time, relative to the beginning of the model's time periods), 2002 with 1, etc.

Next, we define the bond universe U as the set `Bonds` and the associated index, `i`. The bond data are given in the `TABLE BondData` that follows:

```
TABLE BondData(i,*)
                Price       Maturity      Coupon
    DS-8-06     112.35        2006           8
    DS-8-03     105.33        2003           8
    DS-7-07     111.25        2007           7
    DS-7-04     107.30        2004           7
    DS-6-11     107.62        2011           6
    DS-6-09     106.68        2009           6
    DS-6-02     101.93        2002           6
    DS-5-05     101.30        2005           5
    DS-5-03     101.61        2003           5
    DS-4-02     100.06        2002           4;
```

The table's first index denotes the bonds. The asterisk as the second index indicates that this index position is not associated with any underlying set (such as `Time`), but can contain any identifier. In this case we need to specify each bond's `Price`, `Maturity` year, and `Coupon` rate. Although we only need to know each bond's cashflow for each year to specify the model, it is a good principle to specify only the most *fundamental data* in a model, and then explicitly calculate any derived data needed. Hence the calculation of the bond cashflows that follow is based on the fundamental `BondData`:

```
PARAMETER F(t,i);
F(t,i) = 1$(tau(t) = Maturity(i))
         + coupon(i) $ (tau(t) <= Maturity(i) and tau(t) > 0);
```

This assignment is executed for each combination of the indices `i` and `t`. The right-hand side specifies that there is a cashflow of unity in the year where the bond matures, and a coupon payment in every year before the bond maturity, except the first. The statement illustrates the use of the *conditional*, or $-operator: The condition on its right is evaluated; if the result is true (non-zero), then the value of the operator is the expression on its left, otherwise it is 0. For readability we have extracted the bond data from the table into individual vectors `Maturity`, `Coupon`, etc.

Variables, equations, and the model

After specifying the `Liability` sequence and displaying the model data (which causes GAMS to print them to the listing file), we are ready to set up the actual optimization model. The notation `POSITIVE VARIABLES x(i)` specifies that we need variables $x_i \geq 0$ (note that "positive" really means "non-negative"), which denote the face value amount of each bond to purchase. The reinvestment variable v_t^+ is called `surplus(t)`. GAMS requires that the model's objective value be defined as a free variable, so we declare v_0 as `VARIABLE v0`, having no bounds.

We then declare the model's constraints in the `EQUATION CashFlowCon(t)` declaration, and define it (one for each value of `t`) as follows:

```
CashFlowCon(t)..
    (SUM(i, F(t,i) * x(i))) +
    (v0 - SUM(i, Price(i) * x(i)))          $(tau(t) = 0) +
    (( 1 + rf(t-1) ) * surplus(t-1))        $(tau(t) > 0) =E=
     surplus(t) + Liability(t)              $(tau(t) > 0);
```

This constraint states that the incoming cashflow for each year should match the liabilities. The definition of an equation is indicated by the ".." sequence, and $= E =$ specifies that this is an equality constraint (as opposed to $= G =$ or $= L =$ for $\geq$ and $\leq$). Note the use of the $-operator to implement conditions: the bonds' prices and `v0` only occur in the constraint corresponding to time 0; the term `(1+rf(t-1)) * surplus(t-1)` only occurs in subsequent time periods. In this way, the constraint here actually implements both of the cashflow constraints of the formal model, i.e., for all values of t. Note also the use of the `SUM(i, ...)` operator to implement the summation $\sum_i F_{ti} x_i$,

Then we define the complete optimization model `Dedication`, consisting of the constraints `CashFlowCon` (and implicitly the variables referenced in those constraints), and ask to have the model solved, minimizing $v0$ and using an `LP` (Linear Programming) solver. Finally, we ask that the results be displayed: The final values ("levels") of the variables $v0$ and x_i, and the shadow prices ("marginals") of x_i as well as the dual variables corresponding to the cashflow constraints.

Note that, although a formal mathematical model often uses one-letter names, one can use more descriptive names in the GAMS model.

GAMS output

From the execution of source file `DedicationNoBorrow.gsm` we obtain listing file `DedicationNoBorrow.lst`. This file contains a wealth of information. First, the input source is listed. Any compilation errors will be highlighted here:

```
24    PARAMETER cf(i, t);
25    typo(t,i) =      1  $  (tau(t)  = maturity(i))
****      $140
```

The indication is an error 140 at the symbol `typo`; the actual error message appears after the listing:

```
140  Unknown symbol
```

When there are many error messages grouped together it's worthwhile to focus on the first one in particular; the rest are often spurious messages.

Next, we find the output from the statement `DISPLAY BondData, Liability;`:

```
----      86 PARAMETER BondData


                Price    Maturity        Coupon

DS-8-06       112.350    2006.000        8.000
DS-8-03       105.330    2003.000        8.000
DS-7-07       111.250    2007.000        7.000
DS-7-04       107.300    2004.000        7.000
DS-6-11       107.620    2011.000        6.000
DS-6-09       106.680    2009.000        6.000
DS-6-02       101.930    2002.000        6.000
DS-5-05       101.300    2005.000        5.000
DS-5-03       101.610    2003.000        5.000
DS-4-02       100.060    2002.000        4.000


----      88 PARAMETER Liability  Stream of liabilities

2002   80000,   2003 100000,   2004 110000, 2005 120000,
2006   140000   2007 120000,   2008   90000,
2009   50000,   2010   75000,   2011 150000
```

The next major sections are the equation and variable listings.

```
Dedication model without borrowing Equation Listing
SOLVE Dedication Using LP From line 109


---- CashFlowCon  =E=  Equations defining the cashflow balance

CashFlowCon(2001)..


    - 1.1235*x(DS-8-06) - 1.0533*x(DS-8-03) - 1.1125*x(DS-7-07)


    - 1.073*x(DS-7-04) - 1.0762*x(DS-6-11) - 1.0668*x(DS-6-09)
```

```
      - 1.0193*x(DS-6-02) - 1.013*x(DS-5-05) - 1.0161*x(DS-5-03)

      - 1.0006*x(DS-4-02) - surplus(2001) + v0 =E= 0 ; (LHS = 0)

CashFlowCon(2002)..

      0.08*x(DS-8-06) + 0.08*x(DS-8-03) + 0.07*x(DS-7-07)

      + 0.07*x(DS-7-04) + 0.06*x(DS-6-11) + 0.06*x(DS-6-09)

      + 1.06*x(DS-6-02) + 0.05*x(DS-5-05) + 0.05*x(DS-5-03)

      + 1.04*x(DS-4-02) + 1.04*surplus(2001) - surplus(2002)

      =E= 80000 ; (LHS = 0, INFES = 80000 ***)

CashFlowCon(2003)..

      0.08*x(DS-8-06) + 1.08*x(DS-8-03) + 0.07*x(DS-7-07)

      + 0.07*x(DS-7-04) + 0.06*x(DS-6-11) + 0.06*x(DS-6-09)

      + 0.05*x(DS-5-05) + 1.05*x(DS-5-03) + 1.04*surplus(2002)

      - surplus(2003) =E= 100000 ;

      (LHS = 0, INFES = 100000 ***)

REMAINING 8 ENTRIES SKIPPED
```

GAMS lists the equations in the model in a normalized format with variables on the left and a constant right-hand side. For each block of equations (here, CashFlowCon), only a few are listed (by default three, but this can be changed using OPTION LIMROW = n). If a variable's coefficient is shown in parentheses the coefficient is non-constant. This only occurs in nonlinear models, and the coefficient then is the partial derivative, at the initial point, of the constraint left-hand side with respect to the variable. The listing also shows that the initial point is infeasible in these constraints (the initial point is given by the variables' L or "level" values; see Section 1.3.5; of course, this does not mean that the model itself is infeasible!

The variable listing has the format:

```
---- x  Face value purchased

x(DS-8-06)
                  (.LO, .L, .UP, .M = 0, 0, +INF, 0)
         -1.1235  CashFlowCon(2001)
          0.08     CashFlowCon(2002)
```

```
0.08      CashFlowCon(2003)
0.08      CashFlowCon(2004)
0.08      CashFlowCon(2005)
1.08      CashFlowCon(2006)
```

which shows that $x(DS-8-06)$ has bounds 0 and infinity, level value 0, and that
it occurs in six constraints: in `CashFlowCon(2001)` with coefficient -1.1235, in
`CashFlowCon(2002)` with coefficient 0.08, etc. The number of variables in each block
for which this information is shown can be specified by OPTION LIMCOL $=$ n, and is three
by default.

The model statistics show the final size of the model:

```
MODEL STATISTICS

BLOCKS OF EQUATIONS          1     SINGLE EQUATIONS          11
BLOCKS OF VARIABLES          3     SINGLE VARIABLES          22
NON ZERO ELEMENTS           73
```

After solving the model, GAMS displays various status messages:

```
            S O L V E       S U M M A R Y

    MODEL    Dedication           OBJECTIVE   v0
    TYPE     LP                   DIRECTION   MINIMIZE
    SOLVER   CPLEX                FROM LINE   105

**** SOLVER STATUS     1 NORMAL COMPLETION
**** MODEL STATUS      1 OPTIMAL
**** OBJECTIVE VALUE         800237.2480

  RESOURCE USAGE, LIMIT        0.125      1000.000
  ITERATION COUNT, LIMIT       9          10000
```

The important things to note are that the solver terminated normally, and that the model
status is "optimal." Messages about solver problems, about infeasible or unbounded models,
would also show up here. The final part of the standard output lists the model's equations
and variables (only a small part of it is shown):

```
---- EQU CashFlowCon  Equations defining the cashflow balance

          LOWER      LEVEL      UPPER      MARGINAL

2001        .          .          .          1.000
2002   80000.000  80000.000  80000.000       0.962
2003   1.0000E+5  1.0000E+5  1.0000E+5       0.904
2004   1.1000E+5  1.1000E+5  1.1000E+5       0.869
2005   1.2000E+5  1.2000E+5  1.2000E+5       0.835
```

	LOWER	LEVEL	UPPER	MARGINAL
DS-8-06	.	2.7487E+5	+INF	.
DS-8-03	.	1.1710E+5	+INF	.
DS-7-07	.	.	+INF	0.010
DS-7-04	.	.	+INF	0.012

The columns marked LEVEL list the values of variables or constraints left-hand sides, and the MARGINAL column lists dual information. The columns marked LOWER and UPPER list bounds on variables or constraints (the "bounds" and "level" of a constraint are explained in Section 1.3.6). A period in a numerical field means zero. Marginals may be reported as EPS; see Section 1.3.3 for details. Also, in infeasible models, equations that are not satisfied (or variables not within their bounds) are flagged INFEAS. Be aware that the cause of the infeasibility may lie elsewhere in the model.

There are various options to modify the standard output; see Table 1.6.

2.4.2   The FINLIB files

The GAMS source code and data for the models of this section are given in the following files:

- DedicationNoBorrow.gms

- BondData.inc

Chapter 3

Mean-Variance Portfolio Optimization

3.1 Preview

In this chapter we develop the GAMS models for mean-variance portfolio optimization. The development is based on the discussion of Chapter PFO-3. The following models are discussed in this chapter and the GAMS source code for each is given in the associated FINLIB files:

Basics of mean-variance models are based on Section PFO-3.2. We set up the framework to trace mean-variance efficient frontiers. The relevant statistics – expected returns and variance-covariance matrixes – are estimated from historically observed data.

- MeanVar.gms

- Estimate.gms

Sharpe ratio model is based on Section PFO-3.2.2 with the optimal Sharpe ratio.

- Sharpe.gms

Portfolio limits are based on Section PFO-3.2.2. We determine portfolios with a limited number of assets, or minimum proportions, using binary variables.

- MeanVarShort.gms

- MeanVarMip.gms

- Borrow.gms

International mean-variance portfolio management formulates a large model for managing a portfolio of international stock and bond indices.

- InternationalMeanVar.gms

3.2   Basics of Mean-Variance Models

The classic mean-variance model addresses the question of trading off the portfolio expected return against its risk as measured by the variance of return. The model assumes normally distributed returns and multivariate normal correlation structures, but it is also applied in practice when the distributions are almost normal. For more details on the theoretical background of the model, see Section PFO-3.2.

Our first model is the basic mean-variance Model PFO-3.2.3, which we reproduce here:

Model PFO-3.2.3 Mean-variance efficient portfolios

$$\text{Minimize}\quad \lambda\sigma^2(x) - (1-\lambda)R(x;\bar{r}) \tag{3.1}$$

$$\text{subject to}\quad \sum_{i=1}^{n} x_i = 1, \tag{3.2}$$

$$x \in X. \tag{3.3}$$

We have available, in our data set, estimates of expected returns and the variance-covariance matrix for a universe of eight assets: an index of Italian government bonds with short maturity, some stock indices including the general Italian index, and a cash position in Euro as the risk-free asset. We compute the expected returns for each asset and the variance-covariance matrix through `Estimate.gms` (see Section 3.2.1 for details).

The output of `Estimate.gms` is dumped into a GDX container (`Estimate.gdx`), and the data needed are then loaded into `MeanVar.gms` by the GDX utility:

```
SET Assets;

ALIAS(Assets,i,j);

PARAMETERS
        RiskFreeRate
        ExpectedReturns(i)   Expected returns
        VarCov(i,j)          Variance-Covariance matrix ;

$GDXIN Estimate
$LOAD Assets=subset RiskFreeRate=MeanRiskFreeReturn
$LOAD VarCov ExpectedReturns
$GDXIN
```

Note that the SET and PARAMETERS are first declared and then filled via the `load` call. In particular, the set `Assets` is assigned the parameter `subset`. The latter is defined and filled in `Estimate.gms` and dumped into the GDX container. `VarCov` is simply listed, without assignment, since this parameter has the same name as that contained in `Estimate.gms`.

In the VARIABLES section of the model we declare the vector of holdings of the assets. This vector is restricted to be positive since we are assuming for now that short sales are not allowed. In the model discussed in Section 3.2.2 we remove this restriction. Other variables are the expected return, the variance of the portfolio, and the objective function value.

```
POSITIVE VARIABLES
    x(i) Holdings of assets;

VARIABLES
    PortVariance Portfolio variance
    PortReturn   Portfolio return
    z            Objective function value;
```

The portfolio expected return (`PortReturn`) and the portfolio variance (`PortVariance`) are defined by the equations:

```
ReturnDef ..   PortReturn    =E= SUM(i, ExpectedReturns(i)*x(i));
VarDef    ..   PortVariance  =E= SUM((i,j), x(i)*VarCov(i,j)*x(j));
```

The variables `x(i)` measure the fraction of capital to be invested in each asset. By normalizing to one, the set of feasible portfolios – those whose weights add up to one – is identified by the following constraint:

```
NormalCon ..  SUM(i, x(i))  =E= 1;
```

The objective value `z` is a weighted sum of the portfolio's expected return, `PortReturn`, and its risk, `PortVariance`, where the parameter λ varies between zero and one.

```
ObjDef .. z  =E= (1-lambda) * PortReturn - lambda * PortVariance;
```

The parameter `lambda` (λ in Model PFO-3.2.3) represents the investor risk attitude. If it is close to one, the investor is risk averse, emphasizing the risk component (variance) without regard to expected return. When it is zero the investor is risk-neutral.

Different risk attitudes are suitable for different investors. We therefore trace the mean-variance efficient frontier corresponding to portfolios that are optimal for different values of λ. In GAMS, this can be done using a `FOR` loop:

```
FOR  (lambda = 0 TO 1 BY 0.1,
    SOLVE MeanVar MAXIMIZING z USING nlp;
    PUT lambda:6:5, z.L:6:5, PortVariance.L:6:5, PortReturn.L:6:5,;
    LOOP (i, PUT x.L(i):6:5 );
    PUT /;
)
```

This code segment will solve the model for values of λ ranging from zero to one in increments of 0.1.

The results of the optimization are stored in a file by means of the `PUT` statement. The data needed to plot the efficient frontier are the optimal portfolio variance (`PortVariance.L`) and the optimal portfolio return (`PortReturn.L`). With each mean-variance pair corresponding to a given value of λ, there is an optimal portfolio (`x.L`) stored in the same file.

An alternative way of writing and presenting the results obtained is through the GDX utility GDXXRW. In this case, data structures have to be declared in order to receive the output produced. As a starting point we define the set of points that will describe the efficient frontier.

```
SET FrontierPoints / PP_0 * PP_10 /
```

```
ALIAS (FrontierPoints,p);
```

To each point there will correspond a minimum variance, an expected return, and an optimal portfolio. Information about the solver status is also stored. All these parameters have to be indexed by p:

```
PARAMETERS
          RiskWeight(p)              Investor's risk attitude parameter
          MinimumVariance(p)        Optimal level of portfolio variance
          PortfolioReturn(p)        Portfolio return
          OptimalAllocation(p,i)    Optimal asset allocation
          SolverStatus(p,*)         Status of the solver
          SummaryReport(*,*)        Summary report;
```

The optimization model is solved inside a LOOP statement indexed by p, and the results obtained are cast in the SummaryReport parameter.

The latter is "unloaded" into the GDX container Summary.gdx, and the GDX utility GDXXRW will produce the Excel file MeanVarianceFrontier.xls.

```
EXECUTE_UNLOAD 'Summary.gdx', SummaryReport;
```

```
EXECUTE 'GDXXRW.EXE Summary.gdx O=MeanVarianceFrontier.xls
par=SummaryReport rng=sheet1!a1' ;
```

The values of the optimal (expected return, variance) pairs are shown in Figure 3.1. As expected, the portfolios corresponding to high risk aversion (large λ) have the lowest variances (around 0.01), but also the lowest expected returns (around 10%). In contrast, the portfolios for low risk-averse investors have variances greater than 0.5 and expected returns around 23%. In Figure 3.2 we show a set of portfolios for different values of λ. Note that the portfolios with the highest number of stocks correspond to the more risk-averse investors, as these investors diversify their portfolios to reduce their risk.

For $\lambda = 0.1$, only the assets EMERGT and NORD_AM (with the highest expected returns) are held, but as λ increases, the model diversifies into up to five assets, as risk is decreased together with the portfolio expected returns. It is typical behavior for the mean-variance model to diversify into a high number of assets when risk aversion is high. Such a portfolio can be impractical and costly to manage in practice, and in Section 3.4 we give an alternative model to address this problem.

An alternative formulation to Model PFO-3.2.3 minimizes the portfolio variance subject to the portfolio expected return reaching an investor-specified target μ (called mu in the GAMS formulation). We reproduce here Model PFO-3.2.2:

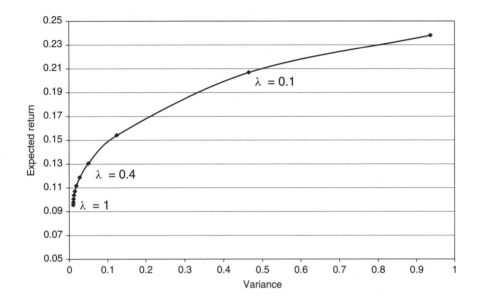

Figure 3.1: Mean-variance efficient frontier when short sales are not allowed. The parameter λ (`lambda` in the GAMS formulation) denotes the investor risk aversion. High values of λ (high risk aversion) are associated with low variances (low risk) and low returns. Low values of λ (low risk aversion) are associated with high variances (high risk) and high returns.

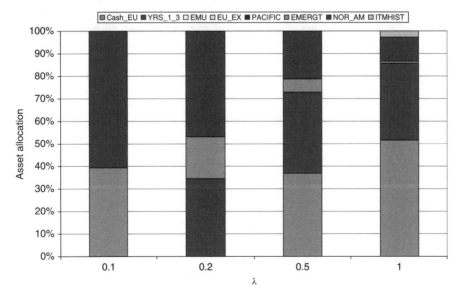

Figure 3.2: Composition of the optimal portfolios for varying values of λ (`lambda` in the GAMS model). As the risk aversion increases, the number of stocks in the portfolio increases as well. Investors with high risk aversion will pay in terms of reduction of their portfolio return to reduce risk.

Model PFO-3.2.2 Variance minimization

$$\text{Minimize} \quad \frac{1}{2}\sigma^2(x) \tag{3.4}$$

$$\text{subject to} \quad R(x;\bar{r}) = \mu, \tag{3.5}$$

$$\sum_{i=1}^{n} x_i = 1. \tag{3.6}$$

The two models are equivalent in the sense that they generate the same efficient frontier by varying lambda or mu, respectively. Of course, the latter model can be made infeasible by specifying a target return outside the range of expected returns given by the underlying asset universe. An example of this alternative formulation is found in Section 3.5.

3.2.1   Data estimation for the mean-variance model

The mean-variance model is usually based upon historical data, such as observed stock returns or stock index returns. We show here how this can be done based on monthly data over a 10-year time period for a large set of asset classes, including the eight classes used in the MeanVar.gms model. The complete data set is found in AssetsData.inc, and Estimate.gms estimates the data needed for mean-variance optimization using the time series of returns. This model extracts the expected returns and variances/covariances data used in the preceding section.

Let the observation times be denoted $\tau_t = (\tau_0, \tau, \ldots, \tau_T)$, where $\tau_0 =$ January 1, 1990 and $\tau_T =$ January 1, 2000, and let $\Delta = \frac{1}{12}$ be the time interval (one month) between observations. The observed prices are first converted to a common currency, the Italian Lira,[1] and stored in the parameter data_ITL(t,i), for each time point t and asset i; the file ExchangeRates.inc contains exchange rates for each observation date.

We first calculate the annualized return of each stock in each period, Ret_ITL(t,i), using the continuous-time formula

$$r_{ti} = \frac{1}{\Delta} \log \frac{P_{ti}}{P_{(t-1)i}}, \quad \text{for } t \geq 1, \tag{3.7}$$

where P_{ti} is the asset price called DATA_ITL(t,i) in the GAMS model, using the following statement:

```
Ret_ITL(t,i) $ (DATA_ITL(t-1,i) <> 0) =
              LOG(DATA_ITL(t,i) / DATA_ITL(t-1,i) ) / Delta;
```

The $-operator serves to exclude references to a non-existing observation prior to the first one available.

The discrete-time version of the formula for calculating returns,

$$r_{ti} = \frac{1}{\Delta} \cdot \frac{P_{ti} - P_{(t-1)i}}{P_{(t-\Delta)i}}, \quad \text{for } t \geq 1, \tag{3.8}$$

might be more familiar; either one could be used.

---

[1] The data used predate the introduction of the Euro, on January 1, 2002, in most EU countries.

Given these returns, it is straightforward to calculate the expected returns over the entire observation period, and the covariances of returns among pairs of assets. Mean returns μ_i, and covariances of returns σ_{ij} (see Equation PFO-2.1 and Definition PFO-2.3.6, respectively) are estimated as

$$\mu_i = \frac{1}{T} \sum_{t=1}^{T} r_{it} \tag{3.9}$$

and

$$\sigma_{ij} = \frac{1}{T-1} \sum_{t=1}^{T} (r_{ti} - \mu_i) \cdot (r_{tj} - \mu_j). \tag{3.10}$$

Note that, unlike the definitions in PFO, we use the historical time periods to denote scenarios, adopting the simple bootstrapping method of Section PFO-9.4.1 for scenario generation, whereby it is assumed that every historical observation is a likely future scenario. The GAMS implementation is given by:

```
* Expected (average) return
PARAMETER MU(i);

MU(i) = SUM( t $ (ORD(t) > 1), Ret_ITL(t,i))
         / (CARD(t) - 1);

* Variance-Covariance matrix
PARAMETER Q(i1, i2); Q(i1, i2) =  SUM(t $ (ORD(t) > 1),
            (Ret_ITL(t,i1) - mu(i1))*(Ret_ITL(t,i2 - mu(i2)))
            / (CARD(t)-2));
```

where i1, i2 are aliases of the asset index i.

From the resulting data, MU and Q, we extract the input data for the MeanVar.gms model, ExpectedReturns and VarCov:

```
ALIAS (SUBSET, s1, s2);

PARAMETERS
    VarCov(s1, s2)
    ExpectedReturns(s1);

VarCov(s1, s2) = Q(s1, s2);
ExpectedReturns(s1) = Mu(s1);
```

where SUBSET is the subset of the assets we are interested in.

The whole input data set and the parameters computed are dumped into the GDX container Estimate.gdx. The latter can be used as input for other GAMS models (see previous section) and inspected, through the GAMSIDE application, to check consistency of the input data and results.

3.2.2 Allowing short sales

We now formulate the mean-variance model when short sales are allowed, i.e., when investors are allowed to sell securities they do not own. In GAMS, the short sales option can be modeled simply by removing the label POSITIVE from the declaration of the variables, x(i), and by allowing negative lower bounds on these variables in order to reflect any limits on short sales. A negative value for some variables in the optimal solution will indicate short sale of the corresponding asset.

The GAMS file MeanVarShort.gms solves the mean-variance model with two types of short sales restrictions: first, only a short position in each individual asset class of up to 20% of the total investment is allowed and second, the total short positions are limited to 50% of the total investments. These restrictions are implemented using negative lower bounds on asset positions in the first case, and accounting for short sales (through Short(i)) for each asset in the second case:

```
* Each individual asset can be sold short up to 20%, and a total
* of up to 50% short sales are allowed.
 x.LO(i) = -0.2;    # Up to 20% short positions in each asset.

 ShortDef(i).. Short(i) =G= -x(i);       # short sales each asset
 ShortLimit .. SUM(i, Short(i)) =L= 0.5; # total short sales
```

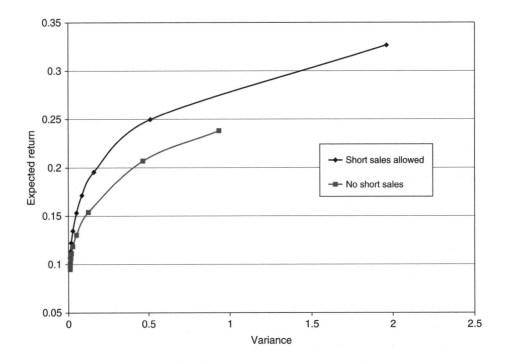

Figure 3.3: Mean-variance efficient frontiers with and without short sales; the frontier with short sales dominates; that is, for the same level of risk higher expected returns are attainable than without short sales.

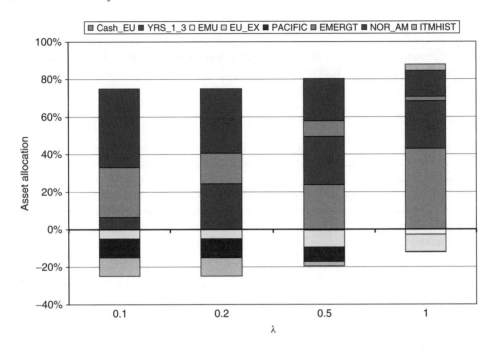

Figure 3.4: Portfolios for different levels of the risk aversion parameter ($\lambda =$ 0.1, 0.2, 0.5, 1), when short sales are allowed.

As expected, the resulting portfolios have even better risk-reward characteristics. The resulting efficient frontier, together with the frontier obtained with no short sales, is shown in Figure 3.3. The optimal portfolios are now better diversified than the MeanVar model (see Figure 3.4), when also taking into account the short positions. Of course, when short sales are allowed, we also introduce the risk of getting caught in a "short squeeze."

3.2.3   The FINLIB files

The GAMS source code and data for the models of this section are given in the following files:

- MeanVar.gms

- Estimate.gms

- MeanVarShort.gms

- Estimate.gdx

- AssetsUniverse.inc

- AssetsData.inc

- ExchangeRates.inc

3.3   Sharpe Ratio Model

The Sharpe model is closely related to the mean-variance model, but maximizes the Sharpe ratio (see Definition PFO-2.8.11),

$$S = \frac{\bar{d}}{\sigma_d}, \tag{3.11}$$

where $\tilde{d} = \tilde{r}_P - \tilde{r}_B$ is the excess return of the portfolio, $\tilde{r}_P$, over a benchmark portfolio return, $\tilde{r}_B$; $\bar{d}$ is the average excess return; and σ_d the standard deviation of excess returns of the portfolio P.

We use as a benchmark index the low-risk Euro Cash account, CASH_EU. The return and variance-covariance statistics are calculated as usual, but relative to the excess portfolio return over the benchmark.

The model in Estimate.gms performs these calculations:

```
PARAMETER
    ExcessRet(t,s1),
    ExcessCov(s1, s2),
    MeanExcessRet(s1);

    ExcessRet(t,s1) = Ret_ITL(t,s1) - Ret_ITL(t,'CASH_EU');
    MeanRiskFreeReturn =
        SUM(t$(ORD(t) > 1), Ret_ITL(t,'CASH_EU')) / (CARD(t)-1);
    MeanExcessRet(s1) =
        SUM(t$(ORD(t) > 1), ExcessRet(t,s1)) / (CARD(t)-1);
    ExcessCov(s1, s2) =
      SUM(t$(ORD(t) > 1),
          (ExcessRet(t,s1) - MeanExcessRet(s1))*
          (ExcessRet(t,s2) - MeanExcessRet(s2))) / (CARD(t)-2);
```

The excess returns are calculated with respect to the CASH_EU, which is assumed to be the risk-free asset. The model equations in Sharpe.gms follow directly:

```
ReturnDef .. d_bar        =E= SUM(i, ExExpectedReturn(i) * x(i));
VarDef     .. PortVariance =E= SUM((i,j), x(i) * ExVarCov(i,j) * x(j));
NormalCon .. SUM(i, x(i)) =E= 1;
ObjDef     .. z            =E= d_bar / SQRT( PortVariance );

* Put strictly positive bound on PortVariance
* to keep the model out of trouble:
PortVariance.LO = 0.001;
```

Notice the need to put a strictly positive lower bound on the Variance variable because it is used as an argument of the square root function. In general, nonlinear solvers will not attempt to evaluate any nonlinear expressions until all linear constraints, including bounds, are satisfied.

The optimal Sharpe portfolio is similar to the optimal mean-variance portfolio obtained for $\lambda = 0.2$. It consists of about 35% Italian bonds of short maturity, about 20% emerging

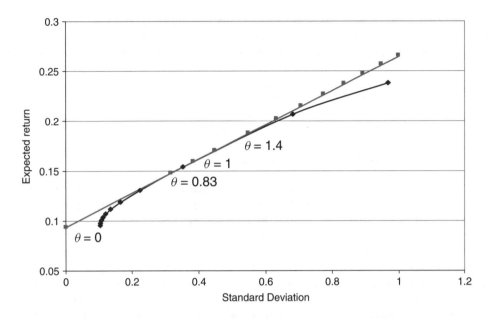

Figure 3.5: Mean-variance efficient frontier when a risk-free asset is available.

markets, and about 45% North American stocks. Recall from Theorem PFO-2.3.1 that this is the tangent portfolio.

In Figure 3.5, we show how the efficient frontier changes once risk-free lending is allowed. The new linear efficient frontier dominates the previous one. The investor will split investments between the risk-free asset and the tangent portfolio fund, identified by $\theta = 1$.

The scalar theta is obtained as the ratio between the volatility of the portfolio, and the volatility of the tangency portfolio,

```
FOR ( CurrentPortVariance = 0 TO 1 BY 0.1,
      theta = SQRT ( CurrentPortVariance / PortVariance.L );
      CurrentPortReturn = RiskFreeRate + theta * d_bar.L;
      PUT  SQRT(CurrentPortVariance):6:5,
          CurrentPortReturn:6:5, theta:6:5/;
);
```

A value of θ less than one implies that the investor is lending at the risk-free rate. Values of θ greater than one implies that investor is borrowing at the risk-free rate and investing the proceeds in the tangent portfolio.

3.3.1   Risk-free borrowing

The amount borrowed can be explicitly modeled in the mean-variance model. Following the extensions given in Section PFO-3.2.2, the relevant GAMS file implementing the model is given in Borrow.gms. We declare two variables, borrow_1 and borrow_2, to carry the amount of money borrowed at two different borrowing rates, BorrowRate_1

and `BorrowRate_2`. Given that `BorrowRate_1` is less than `BorrowRate_2`, in order that
the `borrow_2` is different than zero, we must set an upper bound on the first variable, for
example, `borrow_1.UP` = 2. Therefore, the investor will borrow at the `BorrowRate_1` up
to `borrow_1.UP` and the rest at the `BorrowRate_2`. The normalization constraint becomes:

```
NormalCon .. SUM(i, x(i)) =E= 1 + borrow_1 + borrow_2;

ReturnDef .. PortReturn  =E= SUM(i, ExpectedReturn(i)*x(i))
                - (borrow_1 * BorrowRate_1)
                - (borrow_2 * BorrowRate_2);
```

The normalization constraint shows that all the proceeds of the borrowing go into the
portfolio; of course, the holdings will no longer sum up to one. The return of the portfolio
is diminished by the amount of the borrowing times the relative rates; however, since the
borrowing rates are risk-free the variance of the portfolio does not change.

For `lambda` = 0 only the return of the portfolio is relevant and, therefore, the model
will try to maximize the expected return. This of course can be made as large as we like,
as the amount of holdings increases by borrowing at the risk-free rate. Therefore, without
a limit on the amount borrowed, the model instance with `lambda` = 0 is unbounded. This
is shown in the output file where we report the status of the model after optimization. A
value `MODELSTAT` = 3 means that the model is unbounded.

In Figure 3.6 (left), we show the absolute asset allocations for different values of `lambda`.
Note that the lower the `lambda` (low risk aversion) the higher the amount borrowed and
invested in the tangent portfolio. For example, when `lambda` = `0.04` the amount borrowed
is 4.37, which means that more than four units of capital were borrowed and invested in the
tangent portfolio in addition to one unit of own capital. To confirm that the proceeds of the
borrowing are allocated in the tangent portfolio, we display in Figure 3.6 (right) the relative
asset allocations obtained by normalizing the holdings with the available capital (one plus

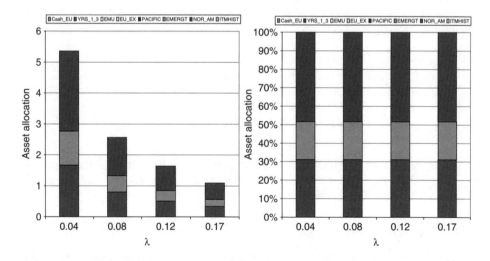

Figure 3.6: Absolute (left) and relative (right) asset allocations for different levels of the
risk aversion parameter ($\lambda = 0.04, 0.08, 0.12, 0.17$), when borrowing at a risk-free rate is
allowed. In this instance, none of the borrowing variables were bounded.

the borrowing). As expected, the portfolio compositions are the same for all values of the risk aversion parameter.

3.3.2   The FINLIB files

The GAMS source code and data for the models of this section are given in the following files:

- `Sharpe.gms`

- `Borrow.gms`

- `Estimate.gdx`

3.4   Diversification Limits and Transaction Costs

A general problem with the mean-variance model for risk-averse investors is that the optimal portfolios often consist of a large number of individual stock holdings, making them very expensive to manage. A natural question is how to limit the number of stocks held in the portfolio. There are two obvious ways to do so: either by explicitly modeling transaction costs and subtracting them from the expected returns, or by limiting the number of stocks held in the portfolio. Such requirements can be modeled quite simply, but the resulting models are nonlinear and contain discrete (binary) variables, and can be difficult to solve. The file `MeanVarMip.gms` contains a modification of the mean-variance model where the number of stocks in the portfolio is limited to `StockMax`:

```
SCALAR
     StockMax Maximum number of stocks / 3 /
     lambda Risk attitude;


BINARY VARIABLE
     Y(i) Indicator variable for assets included in the portfolio;


PARAMETER
     xlow(i) lower bound for active variables ;


EQUATIONS
LimitCon     Constraint defining the maximum number of assets allowed
UpBounds(i) Upper bounds for each variable
LoBounds(i) Lower bounds for each variable

LimitCon   ..    SUM(i, Y(i))   =L= StockMax;
UpBounds(i)..             x(i)   =L= x.UP(i)*Y(i);
LoBounds(i)..             x(i)   =G= xlow(i)*Y(i);


OPTION  MINLP = SBB


SOLVE MeanVarMip MAXIMIZING z USING MINLP;
```

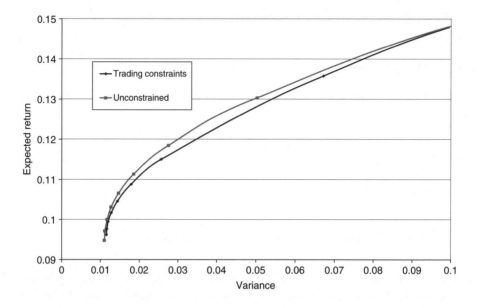

Figure 3.7: Mean-variance efficient frontiers with and without trading constraints.

This is a simple extension of the standard model given in `MeanVar.gms`, whereby binary variables `Y(i)` are used to count and limit the number of assets present in the portfolio. The constraints `UpBounds(i)` and `LoBounds(i)` force the variables included in the portfolio (i.e., those variables i for which `Y(i)` = 1) to stay between the upper and lower bound specified through the `UP` of the GAMS variables and the parameter `xlow(i)`. Finally, the `LimitCon` constraint ensures that at most `Stockmax` different stocks enter the portfolio, i.e., at most `Stockmax` binary variables `Y(i)` can be 1. Note that if short sales are allowed, `xlow(i)` must be set to a negative value; the normalization constraint will ensure that there will be long positions to counterbalance the short ones.

This version of the mean-variance model (`MeanVarMip.gms`) is a mixed-integer, non-linear program, MINLP. For high values of λ, where risk aversion causes diversification, the `MeanVarMip` model results in portfolios with only three assets. These portfolios are usually dominated by those obtained with the unconstrained `MeanVar.gms` (see Figure 3.7).

3.4.1   Transaction costs

Transaction costs can be easily introduced if such costs are proportional to transaction size. In such cases the return constraint is modified as follows (see also equation PFO-3.36):

```
ReturnDef ..    PortReturn =E= SUM(i, (ExpectedReturns(i) -
                PropCost) * x(i));
```

where `PropCost` is the proportional cost. A more realistic setting distinguishes a fixed cost `FlatCost` for transactions up to a certain amount, and a proportional cost thereafter.

In this case the return constraint must include a binary variable to take into account the two cost regimes. To do so, we split the variables in two parts: `x_0(i)` accounts for amounts for which a fixed cost is paid, and `x_1(i)` accounts for amounts for which a proportional cost is paid. The total holdings are given by `x(i) = x_0(i) + x_1(i)`.

We devote a part of the model in `MeanVarMIP.gms` to this case. The new equation definitions are:

```
HoldingCon(i)..        x(i) =E= x_0(i) + x_1(i);
NormalConWithCost ..   SUM(i, x(i) )   =E= 1;
ReturnDefWithCost..    PortReturn =E= SUM(i,(ExpectedReturns(i) * x_0(i) -
                       FlatCost*Y(i))) +
                       SUM(i, (ExpectedReturns(i) - PropCost) * x_1(i));
FlatCostBounds(i)..    x_0(i) =L= x_0.UP(i) * Y(i);
LinCostBounds(i)..     x_1(i) =L= Y(i);
```

Note that equation `ReturnDefWithCost`, which defines the expected return of the portfolio, is made up of two components: one where the transaction fee is fixed, and a second where the transaction costs are proportional (see Equation PFO-3.38).

By setting the transaction costs to

```
SCALARS
   FlatCost Flat transaction cost / 0.001 /
   PropCost Proportional transaction cost / 0.005 /;
```

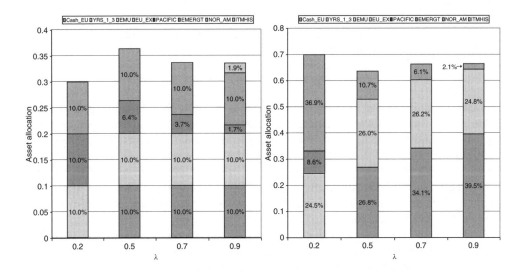

Figure 3.8: Asset allocations under fixed transaction costs (left), and asset allocations under proportional transaction costs (right), for different level of the risk aversion parameter (λ = 0.2, 0.5, 0.7, 0.9).

we obtain the portfolio displayed in Figure 3.8, for different values of λ. On the left, we report the asset allocations relative to x_0(i); on the right the asset allocations relative to x_1(i).

3.4.2   Portfolio revision

In this section we address the problem faced by portfolio managers when, for example, after a change in the parameters of the mean-variance model, they have to revise their portfolio. In such cases, however, one may wish to stay somewhat close to the existing portfolio. Hence a portfolio manager may set a target to stay within prespecified ranges of the current asset allocations.

In the third part of the model in MeanVarMIP.gms we implement zero-or-range constraints, which ensure that the asset allocation will either not change at all from its current value, or, if it does change, the changes will stay within a bounded range near the current allocation. Following the model given in Section PFO-3.2.4 we define the buying and selling variables by declaring:

```
POSITIVE VARIABLES
    buy(i)    Amount to be purchased
    sell(i)   Amount to be sold;
```

The new equations for portfolio revision are:

```
InventoryCon(i)..   x(i) - buy(i) + sell(i) =E= InitHold(i);
UpBuyLimits(i)..       InitHold(i) + buy(i)    =L= BuyLimits('Upper',i);
LoBuyLimits(i)..       InitHold(i) + buy(i)    =G= BuyLimits('Lower',i);
UpSellLimits(i)..      InitHold(i) - sell(i)   =L= SellLimits('Upper',i);
LoSellLimits(i)..      InitHold(i) - sell(i)   =G= SellLimits('Lower',i);
BinBuyLimits(i)..   buy(i)                     =L=   Yb(i);
BinSellLimits(i).. sell(i)                     =L=   Ys(i);
BuyTurnover..       SUM(i, buy(i) )            =L=   0.05;
```

Equation InventoryCon(i) defines, for each asset and for a given initial holding, the total holding, x(i), after selling and purchasing of assets. We split the range constraints in two inequalities, since GAMS does not deal explicitly with inequalities ranges; those are given by UpBuyLimits(i), UpSellLimits(i), LoBuyLimits(i) and LoSellLimits(i). The binary variables, Yb(i) and Ys(i), force the buy and sell variables to be zero or to stay within the prespecified range. Finally, the BuyTurnover constraint takes care of the total turnover. Note that, since the asset allocations must add up to one, the total turnover limits both the buy and the sell amounts.

In Figure 3.9 we show the asset allocation after the revision of the portfolio. The initial holdings are set equal to those of the optimal mean-variance portfolio with $\lambda = 0.5$ and no turnover constraints. By comparing Figure 3.9 with Figure 3.2, we note that the portfolio with $\lambda = 0.5$ did not change. As expected, when the expected returns and the variance-covariance matrix stay fixed or move little, the revision of the portfolio should have no effect. However, if we change the risk aversion parameter λ to 0.1 or 0.2, the new asset allocation will hit the bounds of the selling and purchasing variables.

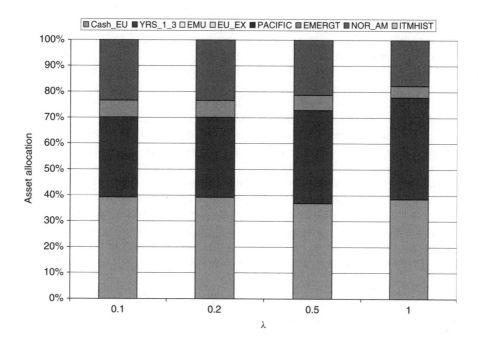

Figure 3.9: Asset allocation after portfolio revision. The initial holding is set to the unconstrained optimal portfolio with $\lambda = 0.5$.

3.4.3 The FINLIB files

The GAMS source code and data for the models of this section are given in the following files:

- MeanVarMip.gms
- Estimate.gdx

3.5 International Portfolio Management

In this section we build large-scale mean-variance models for managing international portfolios of bond and stock indices. The models are based on the entire raw data set contained in AssetsData.inc and ExchangeRates.inc. As seen in Section 3.2, the data required by the models are computed by Estimate.gms, and filled in the proper sets and parameters directly from the GDX container Estimate.gdx:

```
$GDXIN Estimate
$LOAD Assets IT_stock IT_all INT_stock INT_all
$LOAD MAX_MU ExpectedReturns=MU VarCov=Q RiskFree=RiskFreeRt
$GDXIN
```

The raw data consists of monthly observations over a 10-year period (January 1, 1990 through January 1, 2000) of prices of 46 different asset classes, including a risk-free asset. These are 23 Italian sector stock indices and the general Italian stock index, three Italian bond indices, seven international bond indices, five international stock indices, three international cash rates and three US corporate bond sector indices. The risk-free asset is an Italian cash account. The data file also contains a time series of exchange rates between all relevant currencies and the Italian Lira, which is used as the common numeraire.

This model deals with asset allocation among broad asset classes by an Italian investor. Our investor first has to determine the structure of her portfolio by allocating funds in the major stock indices of the Milano stock exchange, and government bonds of different maturities. She then extends the allocation to international asset classes, namely government bonds, and finally invests in addition in US corporate bonds. We will see how the efficient frontier can be pushed out when diversifying internationally. However, we must note that all returns are measured in the foreign currency (e.g., in USD for the corporate bond market) so that foreign exchange risk is not included in this model. We can either assume that our Italian investor hedges currency exposure with forward contracts, or we can be patient until Section 7.2.3 to incorporate hedging decisions in asset allocation models.

The portfolio selection in `InternationalMeanVar.gms` is structured as follows:

Step 1. Include only Italian stock indices; this model contains 23 assets.

Step 2. Augment the assets universe to include bond indices of the Italian market; this model contains 26 assets.

Step 3. Add international stock indices. In particular we added five asset classes representing the major international stock markets, bringing the total number of assets to 31.

Step 4. Incorporate all asset classes, which include six international government bond indices and three corporate bond indices, for a total of 40 asset classes.

Step 5. Include a risk free asset, in addition to all risky assets above.

Step 6. Finally, the Italian general stock index `It_general`, is treated as a target liability. The Italian assets (23 stock indices) are then used to construct a mean-variance portfolio that is highly correlated with the target liability, and thus it tracks (or synthesizes) the liability.

We trace now the efficient frontiers for each step of our models. In the `MeanVar.gms` model this was done by changing the weight, `lambda`, between the portfolio expected return and its variance, but in the `InternationalMeanVar.gms` model we use the variance minimization Model PFO-3.2.2, and set a target return, `MU_TARGET`, which varies from zero to the largest expected return among the assets, `MAX_MU`.

3.5.1   Implementation with dynamic sets

In this section we describe the model in `InternationalMeanVar.gms` and its included data files.

The asset universe set and a number of subsets, corresponding to the different asset subsets used in the models, are declared in the include file `AssetUniverse.inc`. For example, the subset `IT_ALL` is given by:

```
* Italian stock plus bond indices
SET IT_ALL(ASSETS) /
                    ITMSBNK,  ITMSAUT,  ITMSCEM,
                    ITMSCST,  ITMSDST,  ITMSELT,  ITSFIN,
                    ITMSFPA,  ITMSFMS,  ITMSFNS,  ITMSFOD,
                    ITMSIND,  ITMSINM,  ITMSINS,  ITMSPUB,
                    ITMSMAM,  ITMSPAP,  ITMSMAC,  ITMSPSV,
                    ITMSRES,  ITMSSER,  ITMSTEX,  ITMSTAT,
                    YRS_1_3,  YRS_3_7,  YRS_5_7 /;
```

The subsets allow us to change dynamically and in a flexible way the universe of assets that participate in each of the six models. This is done through a dynamic set, ACTIVE, which at any point contains the set of active assets:

```
SET ACTIVE(ASSETS);
ALIAS (ACTIVE, a, a1, a2);
```

Of course, the basic decision variables and constraints are unchanged from the previous models:

```
POSITIVE VARIABLES
    x(i) Holdings of assets;

VARIABLES
    PortVariance Portfolio variance;

ReturnDef ..   SUM(a, ExpectedReturns(a) * x(a)) =E= MU_TARGET;
VarDef    ..   PortVariance =E=
               SUM((a1,a2), x(a1) * VarCov(a1,a2) * x(a2));
NormalCon ..   SUM(a, x(a))                       =E= 1;

OPTION SOLVEOPT = REPLACE;
MODEL MeanVar/ReturnDef,VarDef,NormalCon/;
```

Notice that all indexing in the constraints is done using the indices a, a1, and a2, which are aliases of the set ACTIVE. This set will be initialized to different values for the models in Steps 1 to 5. When it is re-initialized, the aliases a, a1, and a2 change their domains as well.

By dynamically changing the contents of ACTIVE, we are effectively changing the domain of the constraint summations. Hence, before solving each of the five models, the following is executed:

Step 1. Italian stocks

```
    ACTIVE(i) = IT_STOCK(i);
```

Step 2. Italian stocks and bonds

```
    ACTIVE(i) = IT_ALL(i);
```

Step 3. Italian and international stock indices

```
ACTIVE(i) = INT_STOCK(i);
```

Step 4. All indices

```
ACTIVE(i) = INT_ALL(i);
```

Step 5. All Italian stock indices plus risk-free rate. In this case the data set is the same as Step 4.

Step 6. Include the general index as liability.

```
ACTIVE(i) = ITAL(i) or It_general(i);
```

The action for Step 2, for instance, assigns to the active set the assets contained in the IT_ALL subset.

The decision variables x(i) are defined over the whole asset universe, but in any specific model only a subset is used. The default in GAMS is to leave the values of x(i) from the previous steps unchanged as it proceeds to solve the next step. This is unfortunate for our purposes, since when we display the vector of optimal investments, it may appear, for instance, that corporate bonds are part of the universe when our model does not include them since the corresponding x(i) may have a non-zero value from the solution of the previous step.

The GAMS option

```
OPTION SOLVEOPT = REPLACE;
```

changes this behavior so that variables that do not participate in a specific model have their values reset to 0 so that they do not show up in the solution again.

Finally, in Step 6, we include a liability and essentially use the Italian assets to track the Italian general stock index. This model is very similar in essence to the Sharpe model of Section 3.3, but instead of calculating the excess returns and variance-covariances relative to the general stock index, we now use a different approach: the general stock index is included in the portfolio, but with a fixed "proportion" of -1, indicating that it is now really a liability (or a short position). The remaining part of the model is unchanged, except that the sum of asset proportions – including the liability position -1 – now must sum to 0:

```
NormalConTrack ..   SUM(a, x(a))   =E= 0;

OPTION SOLVEOPT = REPLACE;

MODEL MeanVarTrack /ReturnDef,VarDef,NormalConTrack/;
```

In this model, with its relatively large set of assets, the optimal portfolios often contain assets with very small proportions, even less than 1%. This indicates that the model would be a good candidate, in a real-world setting, for the zero-or-range constraints presented in Section 3.4. See also Section 5.3.1 and Section PFO-5.3.3 for an alternative formulation of this problem using scenarios.

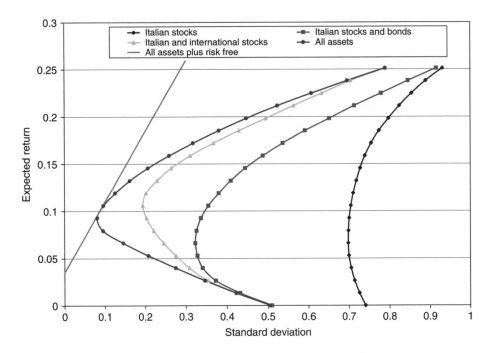

Figure 3.10: Mean-variance frontiers when using increasingly larger sets of assets.

In Figure 3.10 we display the mean-variance frontier for each set of assets. Since each set includes the previous one, the mean-variance frontier dominates the ones obtained by optimizing over a smaller asset set.

3.5.2   The FINLIB files

The GAMS source code and data for the models of this section are given in the following files:

- `InternationalMeanVar.gms`
- `Estimate.gdx`

Chapter 4

Portfolio Models for Fixed Income

4.1 Preview

In this chapter we develop the GAMS models for fixed-income portfolio optimization. The development is based on the discussion of Chapter PFO-4. The following models are discussed in this chapter and the GAMS source code for each is given in the associated FINLIB files:

Basics of fixed-income modeling implements simple GAMS models to perform standard financial calculations, and for bootstrapping a yield curve from bond prices.

- JDate.gms

- DiscreteFinCalc.gms

- ContinuousFinCalc.gms

- Bootstrap.gms

Dedication models are based on Section PFO-4.2. We give models for the standard portfolio dedication with borrowing and reinvestment decisions, and its extensions to maximize horizon return and to incorporate various practical considerations on the portfolio tradeability.

- Dedication.gms

- Horizon.gms

- DedicationMIP.gms

Immunization models are based on Sections PFO-4.3, PFO-4.4, and PFO-4.5. We give models for the factor immunization of portfolios of treasury bonds as well as corporate bonds. Data are given for the US, Italian, and Danish markets.

- Immunization.gms

- FactorImmunization.gms

- FactorYieldImmunization.gms

- CreditImmunization.gms

4.2   Basics of Fixed-Income Modeling

We start with some basic modeling constructs that are encountered repeatedly in the FINLIB models. In the process we develop some simple GAMS models that can be used as financial calculators.

4.2.1   Modeling time

Fixed-income models in general have long planning horizons. Even single-period models, where only today's decision is required, rely on data extracted from a multi-year yield curve or from the prices of bonds with different maturities. The impact of today's decision on subsequent time periods must be assessed, even if this is done in a rather simple context assuming a static yield curve and not allowing portfolio rebalancing. Hence, we need a general way to model time in GAMS.

For all our models we can assume a finite, discrete set of time points where things happen. These time instances represent the stages of the portfolio model. These may be annual, semi-annual, or even some unevenly spaced set of time points. For instance, they can be the regular intervals when coupon payments are received, or they can be the irregular intervals when a liability is due, for example, because a pension fund participant is going into retirement, an insurance claim is being filed, or a construction project installment must be paid. In all instances, they can be based upon a basic set of time points Time:

```
SET Time /2001 * 2030/;

ALIAS(Time, t);

PARAMETER tau(t);

tau(t) = ORD(t) - 1;
```

The actual names of the Time elements are of no importance, and we use ALIAS(Time, t) so that t can be used as the time index. However, we need to associate the elements of the set Time with chronological time. We let tau(t) be the time, in years, relative to the starting date. It will usually be convenient to let the first time point be the starting date, and have the first element of tau equal to 0. For instance, if the element of the time set TODAY denotes the current date, then tau(TODAY) = 0. This parameter may be specified simply as above (for a model with annual stages) or explicitly by the user for a more complicated time structure:

```
SET Time /Q1_01, Q2_01, Q3_01, Q4_01, Spring02, Fall03,
          2003, 2005, 2010, 2015, 2020, 2030/;

ALIAS(Time, t);

PARAMETER tau(t)
    / Q1_01 = 0, Q2_01 = 0.25, Q3_01 = 0.5, Q4_01 = 0.75,
      Spring02 = 1, Fall02 = 1.5,
      2003 = 2, 2005 = 4, 2010 = 9, 2020 = 19, 2030 = 29/;
```

The `Time` set is intended to capture all relevant dates at which cashflows occur or when decisions can be made. Suitable subsets and data can then be defined, for instance, if only some time points are liability dates:

```
SET LiabilityDates(Time) /Q1_01, Spring02, 2003, 2010/;

ALIAS(LiabilityDates, L);

PARAMETER Liabilities(L)
     / Q1_01 = 10000, Spring02 = 3000, 2003 = 54000, 2010 = 148000 /;
```

These subsets can be static or dynamic (i.e., data dependent).

In many real applications, security data such as cashflows, maturity dates, and so on are given using calendar dates, represented by year, month and day of the month. Here, the GAMS calendar functions (see Table 1.4) come in handy in initializing parameters such as `tau(i)` above. As an example consider the following code, where the calendar dates corresponding to time points (`SET Time`) are given by Year, Month, and Day in `TABLE TimeInfo`, and then converted to years, relative to a base date:

```
PARAMETER BaseDate Initialize the base date;

* Base date is January 1, 2000.

BaseDate = JDATE(2000, 01, 01);

DISPLAY BaseDate;

SET Time /Q1_01, Q2_01, Q3_01, Q4_01, Spring02, Fall03,
          2003, 2005, 2010, 2015, 2020, 2030/;

ALIAS(Time, t);

TABLE TimeInfo(t, *) Dates for each Time set item
              Year  Month Day
     Q1_01    2001   01    01
     Q2_01    2001   03    01
     Q3_01    2001   06    01
      ...      ...   ...   ...
     2020     2020   01    01
     2030     2030   01    01;

* Average days per year over the horizon

PARAMETER DPY Average days per year;

DPY = (JDATE(2030,01,01) - JDATE(2000,01,01)) / 30;

DISPLAY DPY;
```

```
* Calculate tau times counted from the base date:

PARAMETER tau(t) Time Tau;
  tau(t) = (JDATE( TimeInfo(t, "Year"),
                   TimeInfo(t, "Month"),
                   TimeInfo(t, "Day"))  - BaseDate) / DPY;
DISPLAY tau;
```

This code is written in `JDate.gms` and a practical example of its use can be found in Section 4.6.

4.2.2   GAMS as a financial calculator: continuous time

With the mechanism for handling time in place, we can now specify some common formulae and expressions used in financial models. As already discussed in Chapter 2, it is good modeling practice to define as little data as possible exogenously and derive all needed data within the model. In this way, if the model parameters need to change we have to change only few instances in a data file and the rest can be computed without the need to change the model. In this case GAMS serves as a financial calculator.

The GAMS models in this chapter use exclusively continuous-time discounting. The source code for this section is found in `ContinuousFinCalc.gms`. Discrete-time calculations are described at the end of this section; see `DiscreteFinCalc.gms`.

Yields, discount factors, and forward rates

The price of a default-free, zero coupon bond that pays 1€ at time τ_t is the discount factor, D_t:

$$D_t = e^{-r_t \tau_t}, \tag{4.1}$$

where r_t is the spot rate; the set of spot rates for all relevant times τ_t is known as the spot curve. Hence, the spot rate r_t is also the yield (or yield-to-maturity), y_i of the default-free, zero coupon bond i. The convention is to consider yield as annualized; i.e., $y_i = 0.1$ means a yield of 10 % per annum.

The GAMS code for yields and discount factors is:

```
   Discount(t) = EXP(-r(t) * tau(t));

   r(t)     = ( -LOG(Discount(t)) / tau(t)) $ (tau(t) > 0);
```

These formulae assume that the yield of an immediate cashflow where `tau(t) = 0` is $y_0 = 0$.

The yield-to-maturity of a bond with price P_{0i}, which has cash payments F_{ti} at time τ_t, is defined as the discount rate y_i, applied to all the bond's cash payments, that equates the bond's present value to its price (Definition PFO-2.4.6):

$$P_{0i} = \sum_{t=1}^{T} F_{ti} e^{-y_i \tau_t}. \tag{4.2}$$

In general, this is a nonlinear equation in y_i, and a procedure for calculating it is given in Section 4.2.3. Note that, for a zero coupon bond with face value 1€ (i.e., $F_{ti} = 0$ for all $t < T$, and $F_{Ti} = 1$), the yield-to-maturity is given in closed form as:

$$y_i = -\frac{1}{\tau_t} \log P_{0i}. \tag{4.3}$$

The forward rate from τ_1 to τ_2 is given by the continuous-time formulae (see Definition PFO-2.4.3 for the corresponding discrete-time formula):

$$f_{\tau_1, \tau_2} = \frac{1}{\tau_2 - \tau_1} \log \frac{D_1}{D_2} = \frac{y_{\tau_2} \tau_2 - y_{\tau_1} \tau_1}{\tau_2 - \tau_1}, \quad \text{for } \tau_2 > \tau_1,$$

and is calculated in GAMS as

```
ForwRate(t1, t2) $ (tau(t2) > tau(t1)) =
       LOG(Discount(t1) / Discount(t2)) / (tau(t2) - tau(t1));
```

or, equivalently,

```
ForwRate(t1, t2) $ (tau(t2) > tau(t1)) =
       (Yield(t2)*tau(t2) - Yield(t1)*tau(t1)) / (tau(t2)-tau(t1));
```

where t1, t2 are aliases of Time.

Present value

Consider a cashflow stream F_{ti} which occurs at time τ_t. The present value of this cashflow discounted according to the term structure r_t is given by:

$$PV_i = \sum_{t=1}^{T} F_{ti} \cdot e^{-r_t \tau_t}. \tag{4.4}$$

A notational difference between Definition PFO-2.4.4 and the above equation is due to the need to give numerical, chronological values to the time index as explained in the previous section. In order to correctly discount the cashflow F_{ti}, it is important to know precisely what point in time the index t refers to. The translation from t to the chronological time τ_t serves this purpose. The present-value formulae are readily translated into GAMS:

```
PV(i) = SUM(t, F(t,i) * EXP(-r(t) * tau(t)));
```

The calculations can also be based on discount factors:

```
PV(i) = SUM(t, F(t,i) * Discount(t));
```

The example model ContinuousFinCalc.gms calculates the present value of a synthetic liability stream, L(t):

```
PARAMETER L(t);
* Now construct an artificial liability stream,
* and calculate its present value
```

```
PARAMETER L(t) Artificial liability stream;
L(t) = 1000 + NORMAL(0,1000);


* Present value of liabilities
PARAMETER PV Present value;
PV = SUM(t, L(t) * EXP( -r(t)*tau(t) ));


* Alternative, using the Discount parameter.
* Of course, we must obtain the same value
PV = SUM(t, L(t) * Discount(t));
```

We show in Section 4.2.3 how to estimate the term structure from observable bond prices.

Discrete-time calculations

Calculations of the yields-to-maturity, discount factors, forward rates, and present values can be calculated in discrete time as well. The discrete-time formulae are given in Section PFO-2.4.

4.2.3   Bootstrapping the term structure of interest rates

A basic problem in fixed-income analysis is that of determining a term structure from observed bond prices. That is, to determine spot rates, r_t (Definition PFO-2.4.1) that are consistent with the prices P_i of a set of risk-free bonds with given coupon rates and maturities, so that:

$$P_i = \sum_{t=0}^{T_i} F_{ti} \cdot e^{-r_t \tau_t}, \tag{4.5}$$

where F_{ti} is the bond cashflow – principal and interest – at time t and T_i is the maturity time of bond i.

Given a set of price equations for multiple bonds i we have a nonlinear system in the r_t's. If, for each t, we are given precisely one bond that matures at τ_t, then the problem can be solved in closed form. The process of recovering the spot rates from a series of prices is known as "bootstrapping."

In general, however, we may have more than one bond with the same maturity or we may have dates when no bond matures. If there are such time points at which no bond matures or makes a cashflow payment, then the system is under-determined and we have to rely on interpolation to get corresponding r_t values. The most common case of course is to have multiple observations, in which case the system is over-determined. In this case it is likely that no set of values r_t exists, so that equation (4.5) is satisfied exactly for all i. A reasonable practice then is to find the spot rates that minimize the sum of the squared errors between the theoretical prices given by (4.5) and the observed market prices.

A simple model consists of minimizing the sum of the squared deviations of the present value of each bond from its price. This is formulated in GAMS by the code segment:

```
VARIABLES
      r(t)                        Spot rates
```

```
   SumOfSquareDev       Sum of square deviations;

ObjDef..   SumOfSquareDev =E= SUM(i, SQR(Price(i) -
           SUM(t, F(t,i) * EXP(-r(t) * tau(t)))));

OPTION SOLVEOPT = REPLACE;

MODEL BootstrapSimple /ObjDef/;

SOLVE BootstrapSimple MINIMIZING SumOfSquareDev USING NLP;
```

In Figure 4.1 we display spot and forward curves obtained by solving model `Boot-strapSimple`. The spot rates show large variations at periods seven and eight, but remain positive for all the maturities. In contrast, the forward rates become negative for maturities after six years, and this is unacceptable in practice.

What we notice from this exercise is that if the number of bond observations is smaller than the number of time points on the term structure, we obtain a poor estimate of the term structure from the above procedure. In practice, it is customary to add various ad hoc constraints to ensure a reasonable result.

For example, we can impose that the forward rates are positive for each time pair (`tau(t-1)`, `tau(t)`) and maturity (`tau(t) > 0`). We translate this into GAMS by adding the following constraints to `BootstrapSimple` to create a new model:

```
PosForwardCon(t)$(tau(t) > 0)..   tau(t) * r(t) =G= tau(t-1) * r(t-1);
```

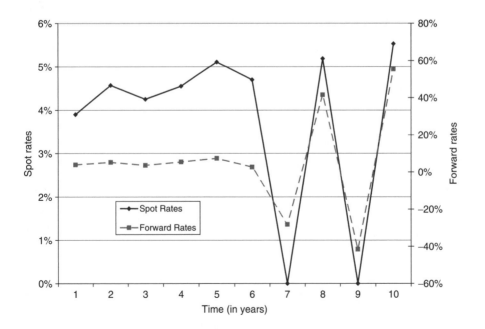

Figure 4.1: The spot rates (left axis) show a large fluctuation but remain positive for all the maturities. The one-period forward rates (right axis) are negative for some maturities.

```
MODEL BootstrapPosForward /ObjDef,PosForwardCon/;
```

```
SOLVE BootstrapPosForward MINIMIZING SumOfSquareDev USING NLP;
```

   In Figure 4.2 we display the results obtained by running model `BootstrapPosForward`
over the same set of bond data used for model `BootstrapSimple`. The spot curve looks
more reasonable now with rates which oscillate between 4 % to 10 %. The forward rates are
positive for each maturity, however, their variation is too large to be acceptable.
   To overcome this behavior, we need to smooth the forward curve such that the change
between adjacent forward rates is small. For this purpose, we modify the objective function
to account for the squared sum of the differences of adjacent forward rates. The term
structure is obtained by properly weighting the fitting error and the curvature of the forward
rates. The weight `lambda` trades off between the two criteria: A `lambda` value close to
one will produce forward curves similar to that shown in Figure 4.2, while a `lambda` value
close to zero will penalize more the fluctuations of the forward rates.

```
WeightedObjFun..   WeightedSumOfSquares =E= lambda * SUM(i,
                   SQR(Price(i) - SUM(t, F(t,i) * EXP(-r(t)
                      * tau(t))))))
                   + (1-lambda) * SUM(t$(tau(t) > 0),
                   SQR( ForwardRates(t) - ForwardRates(t-1)));
```

```
* Recall that the first forward rate, F(0,1),
```

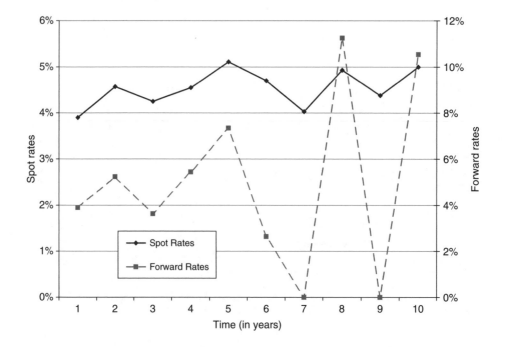

Figure 4.2: The term structure of spot rates (left axis) and of the forward rates (right axis).
Although both rates are positive, their fluctuations is too large to be acceptable.

```
* coincides with the one period spot rate

ForwardDef(t).. ForwardRates(t) =E=
                r(t) $ ( tau(t) = 0 ) +
                ((tau(t) * r(t) - tau(t-1) * r(t-1)) /
                (tau(t) - tau(t-1))) $ (tau(t) > 0 );

MODEL BootstrapSmooth /WeightedObjFun,ForwardDef/;
```

Model `BootstrapSmooth` is solved for different values of the weight `lambda` through the GAMS FOR statement:

```
FOR( lambda = 1.0 DOWNTO 0.0 BY 0.25,

  SOLVE BootstrapSmooth MINIMIZING WeightedSumOfSquares USING NLP;

  PUT "Lambda","Average Error"/;

  totalError = SUM(i, SQR(Price(i) - SUM(t, F(t,i) *
            EXP(-r.L(t) * tau(t))))))

  PUT lambda:3:1,totalError:6:5/

  PUT "Time(in years)","Spot Rates","Discount Factors",
    "Forward Rates"/;

* Calculate and store in a file the results: spot rates and
* discount factors
  Discount(t) = EXP(-r.L(t) * tau(t));

  LOOP (t$(tau(t) > 0),
    PUT tau(t),r.L(t):6:5,Discount(t):6:5,ForwardRates.L(t):6:5/;
  );
);
```

By inspecting the curves obtained from the solution with different values of `lambda` it is possible to select the more suitable solution. In Figure 4.3 we show the forward and spot curves for `lambda` equal to 0.8, 0.5, and 0.3. Note that for `lambda` equal to 0.8 the forward curve looks quite stable with an average fitting error equal to 0.0004.

A more general problem is to find the yield-to-maturity of a coupon bearing bond. Given the cashflows F_{ti} of bond i, the yield-to-maturity y_i satisfies the nonlinear equation:

$$P_i = \sum_{t=0}^{T_i} F_{ti} \cdot e^{-y_i \tau_t}. \tag{4.6}$$

See Definition PFO-2.4.6 and compare to equation (4.6).

The set of equations (4.6) for each i can be solved simultaneously as a square nonlinear system (i.e., having the same numbers of variables and constraints). For this purpose

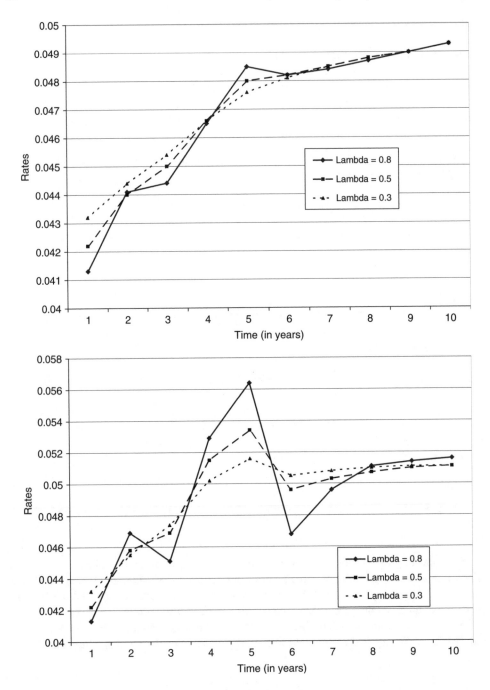

Figure 4.3: The term structure of the spot (top figure) and forward (bottom figure) rates for different values of the parameter λ. The higher the smoothing parameter $1 - \lambda$, the more we penalize jumps between two consecutive rates, and the curves appear smoother.

GAMS provides an optimizer for solving constrained nonlinear systems (CNS). Using `y(i)` to denote the yield-to-maturity of each bond, the following fragment of GAMS code implements the solution of the yield equations:

```
POSITIVE VARIABLES
     y(i) Yield-to-Maturity of the bonds;

YieldDef(i) .. Price(i) =E= SUM(t, F(t,i) * EXP(-y(i) * tau(t)));

MODEL FindYTM /YieldDef/;

* Solve as a square system for the yields-to-maturity

SOLVE FindYTM USING CNS;
```

The structure of the file `Bootstrap.gms` is very simple. The data concerning the bonds used by the model are written in the file `BondData.inc` and they are included via the `INCLUDE` statement.

4.2.4   Considerations for realistic modeling

For simplicity, the models contained in this chapter ignore certain details that are crucial to realistic fixed-income applications. In particular, the models implicitly make the following assumption:

> All cash inflows from the bond portfolio and outflows for liability payments occur on the same date every year.

This assumption allows the use of simple cashflow balancing constraints for each year, but it is unrealistic in practice. While it is possible to use more than one accounting date per year, one usually needs to adjust for cashflows that occur in between the accounting dates that are explicitly modeled.

On the liability side, one can easily shift liability payments to the nearest accounting date by suitably discounting by the short rate. On the asset side things are slightly more complicated. First, the purchaser of a bond has to pay, in addition to the bond's listed price, the accrued interest, which is the part of the next coupon payment that is earned by the previous owner. For instance, if a 6 % US treasury bond with semi-annual coupon payments is purchased one month before a coupon date, the accrued interest is 5/6 of 6 %, or 5 %. This amount must be paid in addition to the bond's listed price, but may be tax-deductible.

Second, when calculating quantities such as present values using discounting, the time until the cashflows occur needs to be adjusted accordingly. For instance, the time until the first coupon payment on the above-mentioned bond is 1/12 year, not 0 or 1 year. Ignoring this may lead to serious errors whenever one is estimating the term structure (as in Section 4.2.3), solving for cheapest portfolios (as in Section 4.3), or solving immunization models (as in Section 4.4).

4.2.5   The FINLIB files

The GAMS source code and data for the models of this section are given in the following files:

- JDate.gms

- DiscreteFinCalc.gms

- ContinuousFinCalc.gms

- Bootstrap.gms

- BondData.inc

4.3   Dedication Models

This section describes the GAMS implementations of the portfolio dedication models from Section PFO-4.2. We reproduce here Model PFO-4.2.3:

Model PFO-4.2.3 Portfolio dedication

Minimize v_0 (4.7)

subject to
$$\sum_{i=1}^{n} F_{0i} x_i + v_0 + v_0^- = v_0^+,$$ (4.8)

$$\sum_{i=1}^{n} F_{ti} x_i + (1 + r_{f(t-1)}) v_{t-1}^+ + v_t^- = L_t + v_t^+ + (1 + r_{f(t-1)} + \delta) v_{t-1}^-,$$

$$\text{for all } t \in \mathcal{T},$$ (4.9)

$$x, v^+, v^- \geq 0.$$ (4.10)

We assume that the stream of liabilities is given by

```
PARAMETER
   Liability(t) Stream of liabilities
   /2002 =   80000, 2003 = 100000, 2004 = 110000, 2005 = 120000,
    2006 = 140000, 2007 = 120000, 2008 =  90000, 2009 =  50000,
    2010 =   75000, 2011 = 150000/;
```

and will be matched through a set of government bonds, ranging in maturity over a time period of 10 years (from 2001 to 2011). All the relevant data are from November 2001 and they are stored in BondData.inc.

Positive variables borrow(t) carry the amount of money borrowed to Liability(t). Observe that borrowing is of course not allowed in the last period – the model has no way of paying back loans after the last time period, and the optimizer would build high debt at the last time period at no cost – and this is handled using the GAMS conditional operator $ on the occurrence of the variable borrow(t) in the constraint CashFlowCon(t), describing the cashflows in each period. We also store the surplus created after the liability is paid, in the positive variable surplus(t).

```
POSITIVE VARIABLES
        x(i)                    Face value purchased
        surplus(t)              Amount of money reinvested
        borrow(t)               Amount of money borrowed;


VARIABLE
        v0                      Upfront investment;
```

There are other such conditions specified by the $-operator, to exclude parts of the constraint at the first and last time period. These kinds of boundary conditions – e.g., that borrowing is not allowed in the last time period and that there is no surplus investment before the first period – are typical of dynamic models. We use here the parameters Now to hold the numerical value of the first year of the model time period, and Horizon to hold the number of years.

```
CashFlowCon(t)..
    SUM(i, F(t,i) * x(i) ) +
    ( v0 - SUM(i, Price(i) * x(i)))    $(tau(t) = 0) +
    borrow(t)                          $(tau(t) < Horizon) +
    (( 1 + rf(t-1) ) * surplus(t-1))   $(tau(t) > 0) =E=
    surplus(t) + Liability(t)          $(tau(t) > 0) +
    (1 + rf(t-1) + spread)*borrow(t-1) $(tau(t) > 0);
```

```
MODEL Dedication /CashFlowCon/; SOLVE Dedication MINIMIZING v0
    USING LP;
```

After the model is solved we can use the dual prices CashFlowCon.M(t) to bootstrap the portfolio yield curve PortYield; see Section PFO-4.2.6. This is an implied yield of the optimal portfolio on the maturity dates of the liabilities.

```
PARAMETER
        PortYield(t) Portfolio yield at liability dates;

PortYield(t)$(tau(t) > 0) =    - LOG(CashFlowCon.M(t)) / tau(t) ;

DISPLAY PortYield, v0.L, borrow.L, surplus.L;
```

Note that the solution of Model PFO-4.2.3 depends on the level of the reinvestment rate that is a stochastic variable. In particular, the reinvestment rate is the future value of the short-term (one year in this case) rate, which is unknown today. We can have better insights by solving Model PFO-4.2.3 for different values of rf(t). In Figure 4.4 we display a set of six portfolios for constant rf(t) ranging between 2.5 % and 5 %, in incremental steps of 0.5 %.

There is a strong interplay between the reinvestment rate and the asset allocation. In particular, for reinvestment rates less than 2.5 %, the portfolio consists of only one bond (the one with the highest maturity), and since the borrowing rate is relatively cheap, liabilities are mostly covered by borrowed capital; as the reinvestment rate increases, borrowing is more and more expensive (recall that the borrowing rate is at spread over rf(t)) and buying

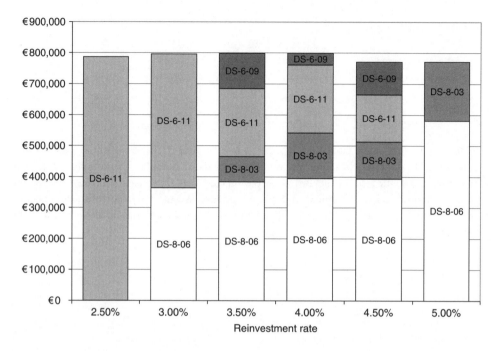

Figure 4.4: The composition of portfolios for different values of the reinvestment rate `rf(t)` shows that when borrowing is cheap the portfolio consists of the bond with the highest maturity; as `rf(t)` increases, the initial surplus (namely, the upfront investment), reinvested at higher rates, is sufficient to match the liabilities.

bonds becomes more convenient. For reinvestment rates greater than 5 %, the portfolio contains no bonds and the matching of the liabilities is obtained by upfront investment reinvested at `rf(t)`.

The reinvestment rate also plays a role in the schedule and amount of capital to borrow. In Figure 4.5 we show the borrowing and reinvestment amounts for each period when the reinvestment rate is equal to 3.5 % (top) and when it is equal to 4 % (bottom). For low `rf(t)`, the proceeds from coupon payments grow at a low rate, thus more borrowing is required in each period to match the liabilities. For high `rf(t)`, coupon payments are capitalized at higher rates and contribute more in matching the given liabilities, and in this case less borrowing is needed.

The FINLIB files

The GAMS source code and data for the models of this subsection are given in the following files:

- `Dedication.gms`

- `BondData.inc`

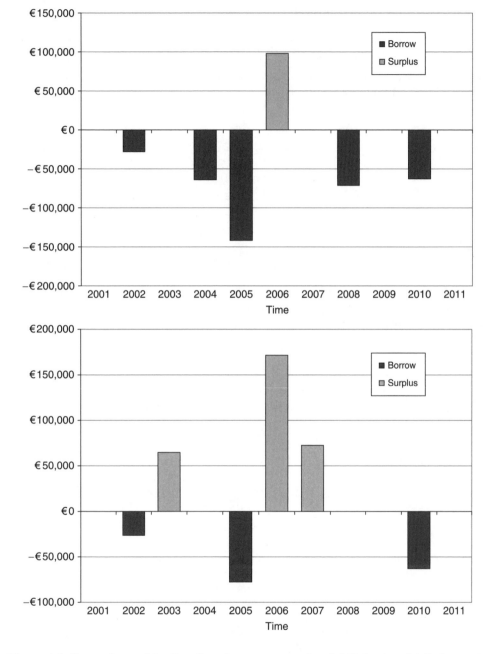

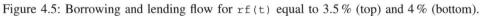

Figure 4.5: Borrowing and lending flow for `rf(t)` equal to 3.5 % (top) and 4 % (bottom).

4.3.1   Horizon return model

The model for maximizing horizon returns is a simple modification of the dedication model, see section PFO-4.2.4. We repeat Model PFO-4.2.4 here:

Model PFO-4.2.4 Portfolio horizon returns

Maximize v_T^+ (4.11)

subject to $\displaystyle\sum_{i=1}^{n} F_{0i} x_i + b_0 + v_0^- = v_0^+,$ (4.12)

$$\sum_{i=1}^{n} F_{ti} x_i + (1 + r_{f(t-1)})v_{t-1}^+ + v_t^- = L_t + v_t^+ + (1 + r_{f(t-1)} + \delta)v_{t-1}^-,$$

for all $t \in \mathcal{T}$,   (4.13)

$$x, v^+, v^- \geq 0.$$ (4.14)

The cash balance constraints (4.12) replace the initial cash infusion variable v0 (equation 4.8) in `BondData.inc` by a given `Budget`. The final period surplus is denoted by the variable `HorizonRet`, which is maximized:

```
VARIABLE
        HorizonRet        Horizon Return;


CashFlowCon(t)..
    SUM(i, F(t,i) * x(i)) +
    (Budget - SUM(i, Price(i) * x(i)))    $ (tau(t) = 0) +
    borrow(t)                             $ (tau(t) < Horizon) +
    (1 + rf(t-1) ) * surplus(t-1)         $ (tau(t) > 0) =E=
    Liability(t)                          $ (tau(t) > 0) +
    surplus(t)                            $ (tau(t) < Horizon) +
    HorizonRet                            $ (tau(t) = Horizon) +
    (1 + rf(t-1) + spread) * borrow(t-1)  $ (tau(t) > 0);


MODEL HorizonMod /CashFlowCon/;


SOLVE HorizonMod MAXIMIZING HorizonRet USING LP;
```

If the initial budget is larger than the optimal objective value obtained by solving the dedication model of the previous section then there will be a positive horizon return; otherwise the horizon return will simply become negative.

In Figure 4.6 we display the final surplus for different levels of the initial budget, and for `rf(t)` = 0.04. With the same `rf(t)`, `Dedication.gms` finds a portfolio whose market value is equal to 798,986€. By using as initial budget such an amount, the final horizon return is zero, as in `Dedication.gms` where the final return is constrained to be zero.

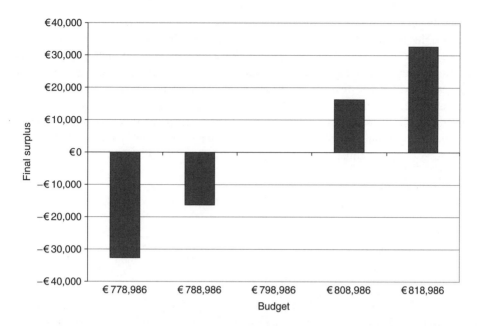

Figure 4.6: Surplus created by maximizing horizon returns, as a function of the initial budget. A negative (positive) final return occurs when the initial budget is smaller (larger) than the optimal objective value obtained by solving `Dedication.gms`.

The FINLIB files

The GAMS source code and data for the models of this subsection are given in the following files:

- `Horizon.gms`

- `BondData.inc`

4.3.2   Tradeability considerations

We now discuss the implementation of some of the tradeability considerations that occur in real-life portfolio management. In Section PFO-4.2.4 three kinds of constraints were mentioned that can be modeled using integer variables:

1. Even-lot constraints, where assets must be purchased in amounts that are "round" numbers.

2. Zero-or-range constraints, where a minimum amount, or none at all, of each asset must be purchased.

3. Fixed transaction costs, whereby a fixed cost must be paid for each asset type purchased regardless of the amount.

A model – MeanVarMip.gms – that implements zero-or-range constraints was described in Section 3.4. In this section we extend the model Dedication.gms of Section 4.3 to include even-lot purchases (with a lot-size of 1000 units), and both fixed and variable transaction costs. The complete model is found in file DedicationMIP.gms.

To address the new features of the problem we must introduce integer variables. As a consequence, the models can be considerably more time-consuming to solve than the simpler portfolio dedication or horizon return models. Even-lot purchase requirements are implemented by adding an integer variable, $Y(i)$, for each bond i, and a constraint that the purchases $x(i)$ must equal $Y(i)$ times the lot-size (here in $1,000€$):

```
INTEGER VARIABLES
         Y(i)             Variable counting the number of lots purchased;
```

```
EQUATION
         EvenLot(i)    Equation defining the even-lot requirements;
```

```
EvenLot(i)..    x(i) =E= LotSize*Y(i);
```

When solving integer models, one should always set upper bounds on the integer variables explicitly. It is important that these bounds be set correctly. Upper bounds that are larger than necessary may lead to excessive solution times, and bounds that are too low may exclude the optimal solution. To ensure that a feasible solution exists while restricting the bounds on $Y(i)$ we estimate the bounds, conservatively, as:

```
    Y.UP(i) = ceil(SUM(t, Liability(t))/Price(i) / LotSize);
```

The model DedicationMIPEvenLot is made up of two sets of equations and is solved using mixed-integer programming algorithms:

```
MODEL DedicationMIPEvenLot /CashFlowCon, EvenLot/;
```

```
SOLVE  DedicationMIPEvenLot MINIMIZING v0 USING MIP;
```

The third model – DedicationMIPTrnCosts – in file DedicationMIP.gms, extends the original portfolio dedication model to include transactions costs. The formulation requires a binary variable $Z(i)$, which takes value 1 when bond i is purchased and incurs a fixed cost of FixedCost, and is zero otherwise. The definition of this variable requires that the $x(i)$ variables have finite upper bounds and those are set up using Y.UP(i) as above:

```
x.UP(i) = LotSize * Y.UP(i);
```

The complete set of additional variables and constraints are:

```
VARIABLES
         TotalCost    Total cost to minimize
         TransCosts   Total transaction costs (fixed + variable)
```

```
BINARY VARIABLES
         Z(i) Indicator variable for assets included in the portfolio
```

```
CostDef..    TotalCost  =E= v0 + TransCosts;
TransDef..   TransCosts =E= SUM(i, FixedCost * Z(i) +
                                 VarblCost * x(i));
UpBounds(i)..  x(i)          =L= x.UP(i) * Z(i);


MODEL DedicationMIPTrnCosts
     /CashFlowCon, CostDef, TransDef,UpBounds/;
```

Finally, model `DedicationMIPAll` combines both models so that we have a portfolio dedication model with limits on lot size and with transaction costs.

In Figure 4.7 we show the optimal portfolios for different combinations of operational constraints and transaction costs. When trading costs are included fewer bonds are included in the portfolio and the matching of the liability is done through borrowing. In this case, as well as when we add operational restrictions, the optimal solution becomes more expensive. Of course, the model will suggest borrowing money as far as this is less expensive than purchasing bonds. The difference in objective function (see Figure 4.8) is an indicator of the price we should be willing to negotiate in order to get special deals from the traders on these restrictions.

Integer programming considerations

When solving mixed-integer problems (MIP) using GAMS there are a couple of points to keep in mind. First, note that GAMS assumes an upper bound of 100 on integer variables.

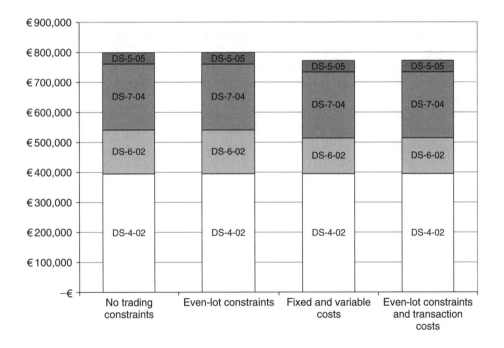

Figure 4.7: Optimal portfolios for different combinations of operational constraints and transaction costs.

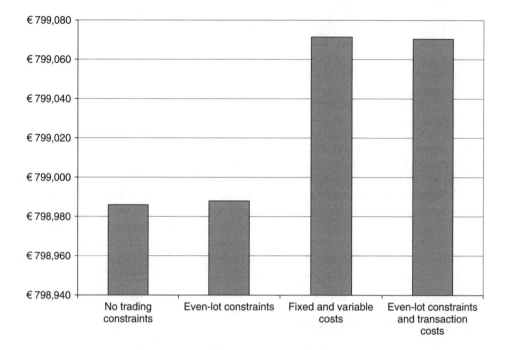

Figure 4.8: The cost of the optimal portfolio of bonds – including transaction costs – for different combinations of operational constraints and transaction costs.

This number may not be useful for some applications and it is recommended that explicit upper bounds on integer variables are specified, using the Y.UP(i) notation.

Second, we must ensure that adequate computational resources are allowed for the solvers to reach an optimal solution, and to do this we set some of the solver parameters.

The following are just illustrative; care must be exercised especially when solving large-scale integer programming models since the combinatorial nature of these problems may make them prohibitively expensive to solve:

```
OPTIONS
        OPTCR = 0
        ITERLIM = 999999
        RESLIM = 100;
```

The first option OPTCR = 0 instructs the solver to settle for nothing less than the optimal integer solution, instead of the GAMS default, which is anything within 10 % of optimal. The limit on the number of iterations is set to a large value, and the CPU solution time restricted to 100 seconds.

4.3.3   The FINLIB files

The GAMS source code and data for the models of this section are given in the following files:

- `Dedication.gms`

- `Horizon.gms`

- `DedicationMIP.gms`

- `BondData.inc`

4.4   Immunization Models

In this section we implement the classic portfolio immunization (Section PFO-4.3) for managing interest rate risk.

Model PFO-4.3.1 Portfolio immunization

$$\text{Maximize} \quad F(x) \tag{4.15}$$

$$\text{subject to} \quad \sum_{i=1}^{n} P_i x_i = P_L, \tag{4.16}$$

$$\sum_{i=1}^{n} D_i^{FW} P_i x_i = D_L^{FW} P_L, \tag{4.17}$$

$$x \geq 0. \tag{4.18}$$

The GAMS model – `Immunization.gms` – again uses the common bonds data set contained in `BondData.inc`, and also uses the (derived) data calculated in `Bootstrap.gms`: r_t, the term structure, and y_i, the bond yields, contained in the parameters `r(t)` and `YTM(t)`, respectively. We wrote the data in a comma-separated format (CSV) and read them using the GAMS dollar statements `ONDELIM` and `OFFDELIM`. This is a very practical way to store data when they are generated by some external software, and it is difficult to write them in the table format (for example, when the input data are made up by more than two dimensions). The GAMS statements for these two files are reported below:

```
* Read spot rates
PARAMETER r(t)
/
$ONDELIM
$INCLUDE "SpotRates.inc"
$OFFDELIM
/;

* Read yield rates
PARAMETER y(i)
/
$ONDELIM
$INCLUDE "YieldRates.inc"
$OFFDELIM
/;
```

The calculations of the basic immunization determinants, i.e., the present value, Fischer-Weil duration, and convexity, are straightforward and follow directly the formulas of Section PFO-2.4.1:

```
PARAMETER
    PV(i)        Present value
    Dur(i)       Duration
    Conv(i)      Convexity;

PV(i) = SUM(t, F(t,i) * EXP(-r(t) * tau(t)));
Dur(i)  = ( 1.0 / Price(i) ) *
          SUM(t, tau(t) * F(t,i) * EXP(-r(t) * tau(t)));
Conv(i) = ( 1.0 / Price(i) ) *
          SUM(t, SQR(tau(t)) * F(t,i) * EXP(-r(t) * tau(t)));
```

The corresponding quantities for the liability stream are calculated similarly.

Based upon these data we define two linear programming models as follows:

```
POSITIVE VARIABLES
    x(i)        Holdings of bonds (amount of face value);

VARIABLE
    z           Objective function value;

ObjDef .. z =E= SUM(i, Dur(i) * y(i) * x(i)) / (PV_Liab * Dur_Liab);
PresentValueMatch .. SUM(i, PV(i) * x(i)) =E= PV_Liab;
DurationMatch ..
          SUM(i, Dur(i)  * Price(i) * x(i)) =E= PV_Liab *  Dur_Liab;
ConvexityMatch ..
          SUM(i, Conv(i) * Price(i) * x(i)) =G= PV_Liab * Conv_Liab;

MODEL ImmunizationOne /ObjDef, PresentValueMatch, DurationMatch/;
SOLVE ImmunizationOne MAXIMIZING z USING LP;

MODEL ImmunizationTwo /ObjDef, PresentValueMatch, DurationMatch,
    ConvexityMatch/;
SOLVE ImmunizationTwo MAXIMIZING z USING LP;
```

The objective here is to maximize a linear approximation of the portfolio yield; see Section 4.5.1 for an alternative.

ImmunizationOne implements present value and duration matching (Model PFO-4.3.1), and ImmunizationTwo adds a convexity matching requirement. As expected, the first model results in a barbell portfolio containing only two bonds, maturing in 2002 and 2011. This portfolio has a convexity equal to 43.237, thus making the convexity constraint of the second model inactive (the convexity of the liability is 34.005). As a consequence, both models yield the same solution.

Model PFO-4.4.1 Factor immunization

$$\text{Maximize} \quad F(x) \tag{4.19}$$

$$\text{subject to} \quad \sum_{i=1}^{n} P_i x_i = P_L, \tag{4.20}$$

$$\sum_{i=1}^{n} k_{ij} P_i x_i = k_{Lj} P_L, \text{ for all } j = 1, 2, \ldots, \kappa, \tag{4.21}$$

$$x \geq 0. \tag{4.22}$$

A possible alternative is to select a portfolio with the lowest possible convexity. As we know, such portfolios are less sensible to parallel shifts of the term structure when the magnitude of the shift is relatively high.

```
ConvexityObj .. z =E= ( 1.0 / PV_Liab ) *
               SUM(i, Conv(i) * Price(i) * x(i));

MODEL ImmunizationThree /ConvexityObj, PresentValueMatch,
   DurationMatch/
SOLVE ImmunizationThree MINIMIZING z USING LP;
```

The portfolio that minimizes the convexity is made up by two bonds maturing in 2006 and 2007.

It is important to realize that no matter how large the bond universe, these three models will never return solutions containing more than two (resp. three) bonds, since they contain only two (resp. three) constraints. Despite the obvious appeal of the simple immunization models this observation points to the need for more advanced models. A significant extension that overcomes some of the limitations of immunization is given in the factor immunization model of the next section.

4.4.1   The FINLIB files

The GAMS source code and data for the models of this section are given in the following files:

- `Immunization.gms`

- `BondData.inc`

- `SpotRates.inc`

- `YieldRates.inc`

4.5   Factor Immunization Model

The factor immunization model is based on modeling and hedging against the primary factors that describe changes to the term structure, as discussed in Section PFO-4.4 and formulated in Model PFO-4.4.1.

The basic factor loadings (Definitions PFO-2.4.13 and PFO-2.4.14), β_{jt}, describe, for each factor j, a specific change to the term structure. The reference by Dahl (1993) provides example data for the Danish term structure, and his data are used in the model below. The data consists of three factors, which together explain 99.6 % of term structure changes. The factors correspond, respectively, to the steepness, curvature, and level movements. The data are given in `FactorData.inc`:

```
TABLE betaTrans(t,j) Transposed factor loadings
          FF_1         FF_2       FF_3
2001      -0.18        0          0
2002      -0.16        0.02      -0.02
2003      -0.14        0.04      -0.03
2004      -0.12        0.06      -0.05
2005      -0.11        0.08      -0.06
2006      -0.10        0.10      -0.07
2007      -0.09        0.11      -0.09
2008      -0.08        0.12      -0.10
2009      -0.07        0.14      -0.12
2010      -0.06        0.14      -0.13
2011      -0.05        0.14      -0.15 ;
```

Given these data, we now calculate factor modified duration and convexity in a way similar to the basic immunization models; see Definitions PFO-4.4.1 and PFO-4.4.2. The duration and convexity data for each factor and for each bond are estimated by the following GAMS code:

```
FactorDur(i,j) = ( 1.0 / Price(i) ) * SUM(t, tau(t) * F(t,i)
                    * beta(j, t) * EXP(-r(t) * tau(t)));
FactorConv(i,j) = ( 1.0 / Price(i) ) * SUM(t, SQR(tau(t)) * F(t,i)
                    * beta(j, t) * EXP(-r(t) * tau(t)));
```

`FactorDur(i,j)` is the GAMS name for the factor modified duration of bond i with respect to factor j, and `FactorConv(i,j)` similarly is the factor modified convexity; similar quantities are calculated for the liability.

The factor immunization conditions are implemented through the following equations:

```
PresentValueMatch .. SUM(i, PV(i) * x(i)) =E= PV_Liab;

DurationMatch(j)   .. SUM(i, FactorDur(i,j) * Price(i) * x(i))
                        =E= PV_Liab * FactorDur_Liab(j);

ConvexityMatch(j) .. SUM(i, FactorConv(i,j) * Price(i) * x(i))
                        =G= PV_Liab * FactorConv_Liab(j);
```

Two models are now defined. The first model contains only the present value and duration constraints, while the second incorporates the factor convexity constraint as well:

```
MODEL FactorImmunizationOne /PresentValueMatch,
                        DurationMatch, ObjDef/;
```

```
SOLVE FactorImmunizationOne MAXIMIZING z USING LP;

MODEL FactorImmunizationTwo /PresentValueMatch, DurationMatch,
                            ConvexityMatch, ObjDef/;
SOLVE FactorImmunizationTwo MAXIMIZING z USING LP;
```

Notice that the duration and convexity constraints from `Immunization.gms` protecting against parallel shifts are subsumed by the factors – in fact, one of the factors is almost a parallel shift. Models like these will generally result in portfolios consisting of at most $\kappa + 1$ bonds to satisfy present value and factor modified duration constraints for the κ factors, plus possibly additional bonds to satisfy the convexity constraints.

In Figure 4.9 we display the optimal portfolios for the immunization models analyzed so far. As can be seen, the simple immunization models – with and without convexity constraints – yield the same optimal portfolio. A different portfolio is obtained when the objective function minimizes the convexity of the portfolio. We are able to obtain a more diversified portfolio when we describe the term structure movements using three factors. Even with this much better diversified portfolio it may still be advisable to add limits on the very short bonds, so that duration drift is limited.

4.5.1   Direct yield maximization

The basic immunization models of Section 4.4 relied upon bond yield-to-maturity and its Fischer-Weil duration to approximate and maximize the final portfolio yield. We show

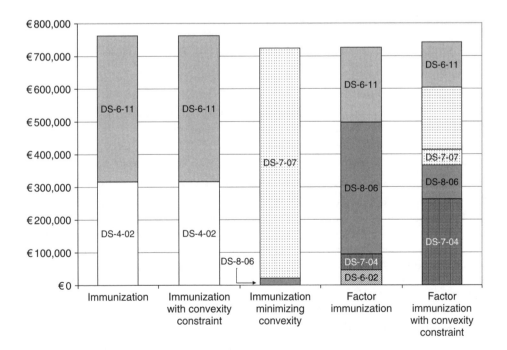

Figure 4.9: Optimal portfolios for different immunization models.

here an alternative formulation that demonstrates the power of nonlinear programming. The portfolio x_i has a total yield y_P which satisfies

$$\sum_{i=1}^{n}\sum_{t=1}^{T} F_{ti} x_i e^{-y_P \tau_t} = \sum_{i=1}^{n} P_i x_i, \qquad (4.23)$$

where F_{ti} are the bond cashflows (coupon and principal) and P_i is the bond price. Our alternative objective is to maximize y_P, called PortfolioYield in the GAMS model given in FactorYieldImmunization.gms:

```
VARIABLE
        PortfolioYield    Portfolio Yield;


EQUATIONS
        YieldDef           Equation defining the portfolio yield;


YieldDef .. SUM((i,t), x(i) * F(t,i) * EXP(-PortfolioYield*tau(t)))
            =E= SUM(i, Price(i) * x(i));


PortfolioYield.UP = 0.20; PortfolioYield.LO = 0.01;


* No convexity model


MODEL FactorYieldImmunizationOne
                /PresentValueMatch, DurationMatch, YieldDef/;


SOLVE FactorYieldImmunizationOne MAXIMIZING PortfolioYield
    USING NLP;


MODEL FactorYieldImmunizationTwo
                /PresentValueMatch, DurationMatch,
                 ConvexityMatch, YieldDef/;


SOLVE FactorYieldImmunizationTwo MAXIMIZING PortfolioYield USING NLP;
```

This model has a nonlinear, non-convex objective function, and as such it is difficult to solve compared to the previous model. When solving difficult nonlinear models it is often useful to provide the solver with an approximate starting solution. This is especially true for non-convex models. In this case, we have at hand the solution of the linear approximation from the factor immunization model FactorImmunization.gms and can use it as a starting point by invoking GAMS with the "save" and "restart" options.

```
gams FactorImmunization   -save FactorSave


gams FactorYieldImmunization -restart FactorSave
```

With this sequence of commands, the nonlinear solver starts off from the optimal solution of the linear program and it is easier to find the new optimum. In contrast, solving from scratch the model in `FactorImmunization.gms` may be unsuccessful.

4.5.2   The FINLIB files

The GAMS source code and data for the models of this section are given in the following files:

- `FactorImmunization.gms`

- `FactorYieldImmunization.gms`

- `BondData.inc`

- `FactorData.inc`

- `SpotRates.inc`

- `YieldRates.inc`

4.6   Factor Immunization for Corporate Bonds

This section describes a practical implementation of factor immunization models for treasury and corporate bonds. The background for the models is covered in Sections PFO-2.4.2 and PFO-4.5 and the GAMS implementations are found in the file `CreditImmunization.gms`.

The models correspond to Models PFO-4.5.1 and PFO-4.5.2, and they cover two credit ratings classes for corporate bonds, AAA and B3. In the first model, it is assumed that the two rating classes are uncorrelated, while the second accounts for cross-class correlation. We begin with the simpler model for uncorrelated rating classes, pointing out however that this is not a realistic assumption. Nevertheless, this model serves as a building block.

4.6.1   The model data sets

The bond universe for the model consists of 13 AAA-rated bonds and six B3-rated bonds. These are used to build portfolios immunized with respect to a liability stream using three interest-rate change factors (shift, tilt, curve). In addition, the basic data consists of yield curves (for the two ratings classes) and factor loading data. The set i accounts for the number of bonds.

The main data are given in the following GAMS data structure:

- `yield(ty, class, *)` contains the term (time) and interest rate for a 30-year treasury yield curve.

- `LiabData(tl, *)` carries year, month, day, and the amount of each liability.

- `BondData(*,i,class)` contains the cashflow of each bond (indexed by i for each rating class), and also their yields, price, and accrued interests. The AAA and B3 bonds are distinguished by the two rating indices.

- `a(tf,class,*)` stores the factor loadings for each bond.

One complication of the GAMS implementation of this model stems from the fact that the securities data (cashflows, etc.), liability data, factor loading data, and yield curve data are all given using different sets of dates. The time set for securities data is called `ts`, and covers 93 time points from June 1, 2000 to April 1, 2010; in `stime(ts,*)` we give a conversion from the time set elements to (year, month, day)-form. The time set for liability data is called `tl` and contains six time points over the 10-year period, none of which coincide with the dates in `ts`. The factor loading data are based on the set `tf`, and the yield curve time set is `ty`. The model uses interpolation to calculate the term structure for each security cashflow date, `r(ts,class)`, and liability date, `rl(ts,class)`. Similarly, using interpolation over time, the factor loading data are calculated from the basic factors to give `sfac(ts,class,j)` and `lfac(tl,class,j)`. These in turn are used to calculate the securities and liability present values, durations, and factor durations needed for the factor immunization model.

The interpolation over time is facilitated by using the GAMS function JDATE, which takes as arguments year, month, and day-of-month, and returns the number of days since the base date. All time points are converted in years, counting from the base date, which is the first liability date. See Section 4.2.1 for an example using this procedure.

To summarize, the following quantities are calculated for use in the optimization models:

- `pv(i,class)` and `pl(class)`, the present value of the assets and the liability.

- `sfac(ts,class,j)` and `lfac(tl,class,j)`, the factor loadings of the bonds and the liability.

- `f(i,j,class)` and `fl(i,class)`, the factor sensitivities of the bonds and the liability.

- `k(i,class)`, the dollar duration of the bonds.

The quantities `sfac(ts,class,j)` and `lfac(tl,class,j)` correspond to the parameter β_{jt} (see Definition PFO-2.4.14), `f(i,j,class)` and `fl(i,class)` correspond to the parameter k_{ij} (see Definition PFO-4.4.1), except that `f` and `fl` are dollar duration. The model is implemented using discrete compounding (with two annual periods) for the securities and continuous compounding for the liabilities.

Model PFO-4.5.1 Factor immunization with uncorrelated credit rating classes

---

Minimize $F(x)$ (4.24)

$$\text{subject to } \sum_{c=1}^{NC}\sum_{i=1}^{n} P_i^c x_i^c = P_L, \tag{4.25}$$

$$\sum_{i=1}^{n} k_{ij}^c P_i^c x_i^c = \begin{cases} k_{jL}^1 P_L, & \text{for all } j=1,\ldots,\kappa, c=1, \\ 0, & \text{for all } j=1,\ldots,\kappa, c=2,\ldots,NC, \end{cases} \tag{4.26}$$

$$x \geq 0. \tag{4.27}$$

4.6.2   The optimization models

The models for uncorrelated and correlated rating classes are described in Section PFO-4.5. We first implement the model where it is assumed that no correlation between the rating classes exists. In reality, the factors used are computed on the whole correlation matrix, so they do take into account the correlation between the AAA and the B3 classes. To overcome this problem, we continue to use the correlated factors, but we constrain the model to allocate the capital available in only one factor.

CreditImmunization.gms consists of several optimization models. The first one, under the name FactorCreditOne, maximizes a linear approximation to the total portfolio yield

$$F(x) = -\frac{\sum_i k_i \cdot y_i \cdot x_i}{\sum_i k_i \cdot x_i}. \tag{4.28}$$

Since the denominator of $F(x)$ is constrained to be equal to the corresponding liability value (i.e., it is a constant independent of the optimal asset allocation), instead of maximizing this nonlinear fractional expression we simply minimize the numerator. The objective function is defined ignoring the minus sign using variable z, and the model is defined as follows:

```
ObjDefOne .. z =E= SUM(i, k(i,"AAA") *
                       (BondData('yield',i,"AAA") / 100 ) * x(i,"AAA"));
```

In addition, the model consists of the constraints, corresponding precisely to those of Model PFO-4.5.1:

```
PresentValueMatchOne ..
    SUM(i, pv(i,"AAA") * x(i,"AAA")) =E= pl("AAA");

DurationMatchOne(ja,"AAA") ..
    SUM(i, f(i,ja,"AAA")* x(i,"AAA"))=E= fl(ja,"AAA");
```

Note, however, that constraints (4.26) are not explicitly set to zero. This is because we can control the equations and the variables involved in the optimization model by simply setting the credit class exposure. As in this case, the exposure requested is only for AAA rated bonds. This approach makes the GAMS model more general. In fact, when another credit risk exposure is required, we can simply substitute its class label with the previous one. In case both exposures are required, the class label is substituted with the set name.

The second model – FactorCreditTwo – corresponds to Model PFO-4.5.2 with correlated classes. We assume that the liability is of class AAA.

Model PFO-4.5.2 Factor immunization with correlated credit rating classes

---

Minimize $F(x)$ $\hphantom{xxxxxxxxxxxxxxxxxxxxxxxxxxxxxxxxxxx}$ (4.29)

subject to $\displaystyle\sum_{c=1}^{NC}\sum_{i=1}^{n} P_i^c x_i^c = P_L,$ $\hphantom{xxxxxxxxxxxxxxxx}$ (4.30)

$\displaystyle\sum_{i=1}^{n} k_{ij}^c P_i^c x_i^c = k_{Lj} P_L,$ $\hphantom{xxxxxxxxxxxxxxxx}$ (4.31)

for all $j = 1, 2, \ldots \kappa,\ c = 1, 2, \ldots NC.$

$x \geq 0.$ $\hphantom{xxxxxxxxxxxxxxxxxxxxxxxxxxxxxxxxxxxx}$ (4.32)

The present-value and factor-matching equations are modeled in GAMS by replacing the AAA labels with the set name class:

```
PresentValueMatchTwo ..
            SUM((i,class), pv(i,class)*x(i,class)) =E= pl("AAA");
DurationMatchTwo(ja,class) ..
            SUM(i, f(i,ja,class)*x(i,class)) =E= fl(ja,"AAA");
```

It is important to note that the models FactorCreditOne or FactorCreditTwo might not be feasible (as is the case for FactorCreditTwo). In such cases, a solution that at least matches the factor immunization conditions could be suitable. Of course, the result is a portfolio with negative entries. From a financial point of view, this means that the asset must be sold short. Fund managers sometimes have the option to hold short positions. In other cases, when selling the bonds short is not possible, a short position in futures could be a practical alternative.

The model FactorCreditThree solves the system of linear equations represented by PresentValueMatchTwo and DurationMatchTwo(ja,class), where x(i,class) is not constrained to be positive. Observe that, without limiting the amount of short sales the model terminates with an unbounded solution, as the objective function can be arbitrarily minimized by shorting bonds. To this purpose, we split the decision variables x(i,class) and add a constraint to bound the amount of short sales:

```
xDef(i,class)..    x(i,class) =E= long(i,class) - short(i,class);

xShort ..          SUM((i,class), short(i,class)) =L= 5000.0;
```

If short sales are not allowed, the factor immunization model must be solved by letting DurationMatchTwo(ja,class) deviate from the levels of the liability factors.

FactorCreditFour accomplishes this task. A set of equations defines the deviation of the portfolio factors from the corresponding liability factors as follows:

```
Deviations(ja,class) =E=
            SUM(i, f(i,ja,class)*x(i,class)) - fl(ja,"AAA");
```

The objective function is modified in such a way that the sum of squared Deviations is minimized, given a penalty parameter lambda:

```
ObjDefFour .. z =E= SUM(i, k(i,"AAA") *
            (BondData('yield',i,"AAA") / 100 ) * x(i,"AAA") ) +
            lambda * SUM((ja,class), SQR(Deviations(ja,class)));
```

In Table 4.1 we show the asset allocation for each model discussed above. Note that the model FactorCreditOne selects only AAA since the variables activated are only those related to the AAA rating class. Model FactorCreditThree matches the factor constraints by shorting a total of 5,000€. Finally, by allowing a mismatch between the portfolio factors and the liability factors, FactorCreditFour is able to select a portfolio with only long positions in both rating classes. This comes at a price, and in Figure 4.10 we show the factors' mismatch in percentage of the liability target. Note how the shape risk due to the tilt factor is very poorly matched by the selected portfolio.

Table 4.1: Portfolios of bonds for the three credit factor models.

	FactorCredit One	FactorCredit Three	FactorCredit Four
Bond-6.AAA		1,300.63€	
Bond-7.AAA			945.59€
Bond-8.AAA	55.20€		152.27€
Bond-10.AAA	45.51€	103.79€	
Bond-12.AAA	796.64€	295.04€	
Bond-13.AAA	672.16€		
Bond-1.B3		−1,306.48€	
Bond-2.B3		−450.12€	
Bond-4.B3		4,948.19€	371.66€
Bond-5.B3		−3,243.40€	473.02€
Bond-6.B3		−597.74€	

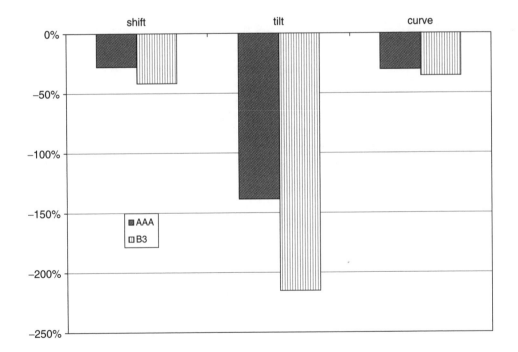

Figure 4.10: Percentage mismatch between the portfolio factors and the liability target factor values. The portfolio selected by means of FactorCreditFour is exposed to tilt risk.

4.6.3   The FINLIB files

The GAMS source code and data for the models of this section are given in the following files:

- `CreditImmunization.gms`

- `TimeDefinitionSets.inc`

- `CreditYieldRates.inc`

- `BondAndLiabilityData.inc`

- `FactorLoadings.inc`

Chapter 5

Scenario Optimization

5.1 Preview

In this chapter we develop the GAMS models for scenario-based portfolio optimization. The development is based on the discussion of Chapter PFO-5. The following models are discussed in this chapter and the GAMS source code for each is given in the associated FINLIB files:

Mean absolute deviation (MAD) models are based on Section PFO-5.3. We give models which select a portfolio by minimizing the mean absolute deviation from a reference point or a target liability. We also provide a tracking model where the target is a market index.

- MAD.gms

- TrackingMAD.gms

Regret models are based on Section PFO-5.4. In this case the risk function is measured in terms of negative deviations from a benchmark; we also use the model to highlight the differences with MAD tracking models.

- Regret.gms

Conditional Value−at−Risk (CVaR) models are based on Section PFO-5.5 and optimize CVaR, which has the nice property of being a coherent risk measure.

- CVaR.gms

Expected utility maximization models are based on Section PFO-5.6 and maximize the expected value of investors' utility.

- Utility.gms

Put/call efficient frontier models are based on Section PFO-5.7. We build put/call efficient frontiers and show the effects of liquidity constraints.

- PutCall.gms

5.2   Data sets

The GAMS models of this chapter are set up using three common data sets. As far as possible identical data are used in setting up the models so that users can compare and contrast the results. The data sets are given in the following files:

- `Corporate.inc`, contains simulated return data for 17 bonds and a risk-free asset, for 1000 scenarios.

- `WorldIndices.inc`, contains 10-year monthly return data for 13 asset classes, including several stock and bond indices from the international markets for 120 scenarios.

- `Index.inc`, contains 10-year monthly return data of an index constructed by averaging the returns of the 13 asset classes in `WorldIndices.inc`.

The models implemented in this section are designed in such a way that it is irrelevant if they are based on a view of the scenarios using forward-looking simulations, or if they use samples from historical time series. Scenario generation methods are described in Chapter PFO-9, and here we take the scenario data as given input.

The data files used by the models are controlled by the GAMS INCLUDE command:

```
* Uncomment one of the following lines to include a data file

* $INCLUDE "Corporate.inc"
* $INCLUDE "WorldIndices.inc"
```

The data files contain simple two-dimensional data, corresponding to asset returns for each scenario. As an example we show here a fragment of `Corporates.inc`:

```
SET Assets      /RF, AA_1 * AA_17/;
SET Scenarios  /SS_1 * SS_1000 /;
ALIAS (Assets, i);
ALIAS (Scenarios, l);
PARAMETER AssetReturns(i,l)  Returns for each asset i and scenario l
/AA_1.SS_1        0.04992,
 AA_1.SS_2        0.04036,
 AA_1.SS_3        0.04193,
 AA_1.SS_4        0.02602,
 AA_1.SS_5        0.01817,
 . . . . .        . . . .
```

The data structure is consistent with a single-period model, as opposed to the multi-period models we will develop in the next chapter. Furthermore, the use of aliases allows us to build GAMS models that are quite general and can be run with different data sets. In other words, it is not the name of the set, but the names of the aliases that will be used in the model equations.

5.2.1   The FINLIB files

The GAMS data for the models of this section are given in the following files:

- WorldIndices.inc

- Corporate.inc

- Index.inc

5.3   Mean Absolute Deviation Models

We develop in this section some variants of the mean absolute deviation (MAD) models, Model PFO-5.3.1 (MAD.gms) and Model PFO-5.3.5 (TrackingMAD.gms). We start from the general MAD minimization model and we repeated it here:

Model PFO-5.3.1 Minimization of mean absolute deviation

$$\text{Minimize} \sum_{l \in \Omega} p^l y^l \tag{5.1}$$

$$\text{subject to} \sum_{i=1}^{n} \overline{P}_i x_i \geq \mu V_0, \tag{5.2}$$

$$y^l \geq V(x; P^l) - V(x; \overline{P}), \qquad \text{for all } l \in \Omega, \tag{5.3}$$

$$y^l \geq V(x; \overline{P}) - V(x; P^l), \qquad \text{for all } l \in \Omega, \tag{5.4}$$

$$\sum_{i=1}^{n} P_{0i} x_i = V_0, \tag{5.5}$$

$$x \in X. \tag{5.6}$$

Note that the model is defined here using asset values (or prices) whereas the scenario data are asset returns. Hence, the model implemented in GAMS uses the value of one unit invested in an asset. Without loss of generality, we also assume that the initial prices (P_{0i}) are all equal to 1.

The annualized returns are stored in the parameter AssetReturns(i,l) denoting the return of asset i in scenario l. The decision variables are x(i), the holdings in stock i. Note that these are not fractions of total holdings as was the case in the mean-variance model, but are expressed in face value and are constrained by a given nominal budget.

```
SCALARS
        Budget          Nominal investment budget
        ....
EQUATIONS
        BudgetCon       Equation defining the budget constraint
        ....
BudgetCon ..            SUM(i, x(i)) =E= Budget;
```

In this model, the scenarios are considered to be equally likely, and their probabilities are declared and initialized as follows:

```
PARAMETERS
    pr(l)           Scenario probability
    ....
pr(l) = 1.0 / CARD(l);
```

Note that, since we are using a large number of scenarios, the above assumption is not restrictive. We are treating our sample as a statistical sample drawn from a given population or distribution function, and the larger the number of scenarios, the better is the approximation of the underlying distribution.

To calculate the mean absolute deviation of the portfolio, we first need to keep track of the values of each asset in each scenario, `P(i,l)`. We also compute and store in `EP(l)` the expected value of each security.

These are defined in GAMS as:

```
PARAMETERS
    ....
    P(i,l)          Final values
    EP(i)           Expected final values;
...
P(i,l) = 1 + AssetReturns ( i, l );
EP(i) = SUM(l, pr(l) * P(i,l));
```

The mean absolute deviation is defined by the scenario-dependent variables `y(l)`. They measure the absolute deviation of the portfolio, under each scenario, from its expected value (see Equations PFO-5.25–PFO-5.26). The corresponding equations in GAMS are given as follow:

```
EQUATIONS
    yPosDef(l)      Equations defining the positive deviations
    yNegDef(l)      Equations defining the negative deviations;

yPosDef(l) ..
    y(l) =G= SUM(i, P(i,l) * x(i)) - SUM(i, EP(i) * x(i));

yNegDef(l) ..
    y(l) =G= SUM(i, EP(i) * x(i)) - SUM(i, P(i,l) * x(i));
```

The objective function is defined as the average, over all scenarios, of the deviations `y(l)`; this is an estimate of the portfolio mean absolute deviation.

To build the efficient frontier of MAD vs expected return, we minimize the MAD objective function and constrain our portfolio to have an expected value greater or equal to a given target return (`MU_TARGET`). We do this in a FOR loop where the target return is increased from the lowest to the highest attainable expected return:

```
ReturnCon ..   SUM(i, EP(i) * x(i)) =G= MU_TARGET * Budget;
```

```
ObjDef..        z =E= SUM(l, pr(l) * y(l));

MODEL MeanAbsoluteDeviation /BudgetCon, ReturnCon,
                            yPosDef, yNegDef, ObjDef/;

FOR (MU_TARGET = MIN_MU TO MAX_MU BY MU_STEP,
     SOLVE MeanAbsoluteDeviation MINIMIZING z USING LP;
);
```

The model shown weighs over- and under-performance equally. Model PFO-5.3.3 shows how to differentially penalize downside from upside deviations:

Model PFO-5.3.3 Upside potential and downside risk in mean absolute deviation

---

$$\text{Minimize} \quad \sum_{l \in \Omega} p^l y^l \tag{5.7}$$

$$\text{subject to} \quad \sum_{i=1}^{n} \overline{P}_i x_i \geq \mu V_0, \tag{5.8}$$

$$y^l \geq \lambda_u \left[V(x; P^l) - V(x; \overline{P}) \right], \qquad \text{for all } l \in \Omega, \tag{5.9}$$

$$y^l \geq \lambda_d \left[V(x; \overline{P}) - V(x; P^l) \right], \qquad \text{for all } l \in \Omega, \tag{5.10}$$

$$\sum_{i=1}^{n} P_{0i} x_i = V_0, \tag{5.11}$$

$$x \in X. \tag{5.12}$$

We rework the related GAMS equations as follows:

```
yPosWeightDef(l) ..     y(l) =G= lambdaPos * (SUM(i, P(i,l) * x(i))
                        - SUM(i, EP(i) * x(i)));
yNegWeightDef(l) ..     y(l) =G= lambdaNeg * (SUM(i, EP(i) * x(i))
                        - SUM(i, P(i,l) * x(i)));
```

where `lambdaPos` and `lambdaNeg` are suitably declared weights.

As shown in Section PFO-5.3.2, when the deviation is measured with respect to the expected value of the portfolios, Model PFO-5.3.3 is equivalent to Model PFO-5.3.1. This is demonstrated by the results obtained from running the two models and inspecting the portfolios for each target returns.

5.3.1   Downside risk and tracking models

In `TrackingMAD.gms` we deal with models exploiting the MAD feature of penalizing differently downside from upside risk. We are interested in placing a limit on shortfalls with respect to the portfolio expected value or to a given target. The target could be stochastic and, if the target is a market index, the model is also known as a tracking model, yielding a tracking portfolio.

Given a user-specified tolerance, ε, the portfolio that maximizes the expected return, and places a limit on deviation below the portfolio expected value, is given in Model PFO-5.3.4:

Model PFO-5.3.4 Portfolio optimization with limits on maximum downside risk

---

$$\text{Maximize} \quad \sum_{i=1}^{n} \overline{P}_i x_i \tag{5.13}$$

$$V(x; P^l) \geq V(x; \overline{P}) - \varepsilon V_0, \qquad \text{for all } l \in \Omega, \tag{5.14}$$

$$\sum_{i=1}^{n} P_{0i} x_i = V_0, \tag{5.15}$$

$$x \in X. \tag{5.16}$$

However, instead of solving Model PFO-5.3.4 for a specific tolerance, it is preferable to build an efficient frontier to trade-off the downside error against the expected return. The larger the value of the allowed shortfall, the higher the expected return attainable. Investors will decide the acceptable deviations from the target, but consistency with the goal of tracking an index dictates that ε should be made as small as possible.

To implement this model, we declare the scalar EpsTolerance and set it to a high value; EpsTolerance is then reduced for as long as the model yields a feasible solution. We use the GAMS WHILE statement to solve recursively Model PFO-5.3.4, and check for infeasibility from the status returned by the model extension MODELSTAT.

The main changes with respect to MAD.gms are reported here:

```
ToleranceCon(l)  ..    SUM(i, P(i,l) * x(i)) =G= SUM(i, EP(i) * x(i))
                       - EpsTolerance * Budget;
ObjDef ..              z =E= SUM(i, x(i) * EP(i));

MODEL  DownsideBound /BudgetCon, ToleranceCon, ObjDef/;
DownsideBound.MODELSTAT = 1;
EpsTolerance = 0.2;

WHILE ( DownsideBound.MODELSTAT <= 2,
    SOLVE DownsideBound MAXIMIZING z USING LP;
    EpsTolerance = EpsTolerance - 0.01;
);
```

If the model terminates with an optimal or locally optimal solution, then the model name extension MODELSTAT returns 1 or 2 and the WHILE loop is continued. If the model is infeasible, the value 4 is returned and the loop terminates.

Extending Model PFO-5.3.4 to tracking a constant target, or a stochastic index, is straightforward. We simply replace the expected value in equation (5.14) with the desired target g, or with the index values under each scenario g^l:

Model PFO-5.3.5 Tracking model

$$\text{Maximize} \quad \sum_{i=1}^{n} \overline{P}_i x_i \tag{5.17}$$

$$\text{subject to} \quad V(x; P^l) \geq g^l - \varepsilon V_0, \qquad \text{for all } l \in \Omega, \tag{5.18}$$

$$\sum_{i=1}^{n} P_{0i} x_i = V_0, \tag{5.19}$$

$$x \in X. \tag{5.20}$$

In `TrackingMAD.gms` we modify the `ToleranceCon(l)` equations to take into account the constant target portfolio return or the market index. Note that both targets must be consistent with the scenario used. There is no hope of attaining a monthly 10 % target when the assets used return an average 3 % per month; indeed, the model will yield a feasible solution only for large downside deviations.

The example in `TrackingMAD.gms` is set up using the `WorldIndices.inc` data. We select a fixed target equal to 2 %, and include a target index (`Index.inc`) obtained as a simple average of the 13 assets contained in `WorldIndices.inc`. Note that if we set the tolerance equal to zero the model produces a portfolio with holdings in each asset identical to the composition of the equally weighted target index. Of course, this portfolio is of no practical use as the transaction costs and the managing costs will deplete the performance.

The main changes in the GAMS code are reported here:

```
PARAMETER
     TargetIndex(l)    Target index returns;

TrackingCon(l) ..    SUM(i, P(i,l) * x(i)) =G=
                     ( TargetIndex(l) - EpsTolerance ) * Budget;

MODEL  TrackingMAD /BudgetCon, TrackingCon, ObjDef/;
```

In Figure 5.1 we display the trade-off between tolerance and expected return. The tolerance is given in absolute value (`EpsTolerance * Budget`), and is computed for different fixed-target portfolio returns (`TargetIndex(l) = K`). For `TargetIndex(l) = 0.10` (10 % of the budget), the efficient frontier is made up by very few points. This occurs because the expected returns of the assets available range between 0.2 % to 1.3 %, and therefore, it is very difficult to achieve the 10 % target unless a high tolerance is allowed, which of course means that the target is not met.

5.3.2   Comparing mean-variance and mean absolute deviation

We now compare the results of the mean-variance optimization model (MV) from Section 3.2, to the results of minimizing the mean absolute deviation (MAD). For a given target expected return, the MAD model minimizes the portfolio mean absolute deviation around its expected return, while the mean-variance model minimizes the variance of the portfolio return.

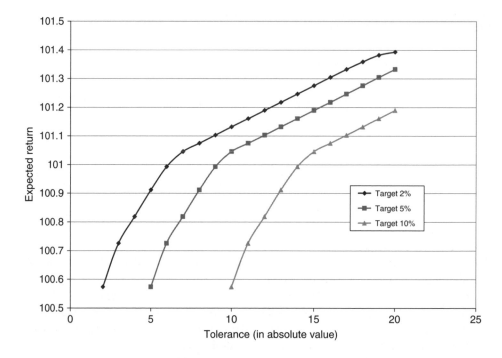

Figure 5.1: Tolerance (in absolute value) vs expected return for a fixed target equal to 2%, 5%, and 10%. Higher target returns are difficult to meet, producing a more restricted efficient frontier.

According to Theorem PFO-2.3.2, the MAD and variance of a portfolio are closely related, provided the asset universe has multivariate normally distributed returns. The relation between the MAD $w(x)$ and the variance $\sigma(x)$ is given by:

$$w(x) = \sqrt{\frac{2}{\pi}}\, \sigma(x). \tag{5.21}$$

This means that MV and MAD models, for identical target returns, will return similar portfolios, and that the MAD and the variance values of those portfolios will satisfy equation (5.21).

We can easily verify this observation using both data sets provided. The details of the implementation are given in `MAD.gms`. We first calculated the mean and the variance-covariance matrix of the asset returns from the given scenario data to solve the MV model, and then solved the MAD model using directly the scenario data for each level of the target return. The results are stored in `MADvsMV.csv`.

In Figure 5.2 we show the efficient frontier obtained with the MAD model and its counterpart using equation (5.21).

Note that the two curves mostly overlap and are only slightly different for the high-risk portfolios. The difference is attributed to the fact that the returns from our sample data are only approximately normally distributed due to the small sample size. This, together with

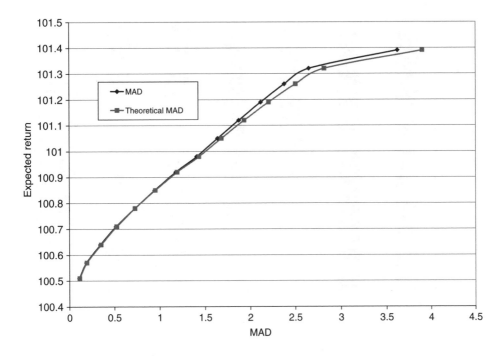

Figure 5.2: MAD efficient frontier and MAD vs expected return for the mean-variance efficient portfolios as given by equation (5.21). The two frontiers are identical, within numerical errors, confirming the relation between MAD and variance.

the fat tails that characterize the stock market returns in our data, cause violations of the formula given in (5.21). The results in this figure imply that the portfolios obtained with the two models should be similar.

Indeed, in Figure 5.3 we show a sample of portfolios with the same target expected return. We observe that the asset allocations are fairly similar and their differences are negligible. This has practical significance because it means that MAD, which is a linear programming model, can be used instead of the more difficult, quadratic mean-variance model. Of course, this can be appreciated for large-scale models with thousands of variables. Furthermore, as variance and covariance data are usually estimated from historical data (i.e., scenarios) these can be used directly by MAD, bypassing the variance/covariance calculations.

5.3.3   The FINLIB files

The GAMS source code and data for the models of this section are given in the following files:

- MAD.gms

- TrackingMAD.gms

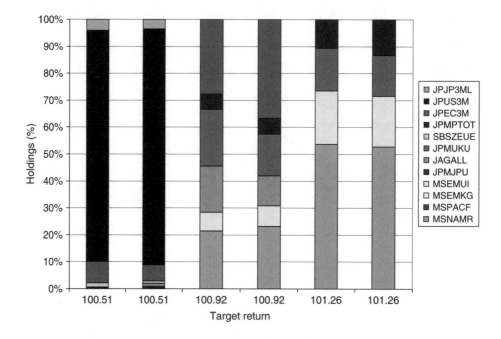

Figure 5.3: Portfolios obtained by solving the MAD and MV model for the same level of the target return. MV and MAD models yield the same portfolio when the return distribution is multivariate normal. Deviations are due to fat tails or small sample size.

5.4   Regret Models

The model to minimize expected regret, Model PFO-5.4.1, is similar to the MAD models of the previous section and is repeated here:

Model PFO-5.4.1 Minimization of expected downside regret

$$\text{Minimize} \quad \sum_{l \in \Omega} p^l y^l_- \tag{5.22}$$

$$\text{subject to} \quad \sum_{i=1}^{n} \overline{P}_i x_i \geq \mu V_0, \tag{5.23}$$

$$y^l_- \geq g^l - V(x; P^l), \qquad \text{for all } l \in \Omega, \tag{5.24}$$

$$y^l_- \geq 0, \qquad \text{for all } l \in \Omega, \tag{5.25}$$

$$\sum_{i=1}^{n} P_{0i} x_i = V_0, \tag{5.26}$$

$$x \in X. \tag{5.27}$$

Indeed, by setting $\lambda_u = 0$, $\lambda_d = 1$, and $g^l = V(x, \overline{P})$, we obtain Model PFO-5.3.3.

A different formulation of the regret model allows deviations from the target up to a given threshold εV_0. We give here the formulation of the ε-regret Model PFO-5.4.3, where, instead of minimizing the expected regret, we constrain the expected regret while maximizing the expected return:

Model PFO-5.4.3 Portfolio optimization with ε-regret constraints

---

$$\text{Maximize } \sum_{i=1}^{n} \overline{P}_i x_i \tag{5.28}$$

$$\text{subject to } \sum_{l \in \Omega} p^l y_-^l \leq \omega, \tag{5.29}$$

$$y_-^l \geq (g^l - \varepsilon V_0) - V(x; P^l), \qquad \text{for all } l \in \Omega, \tag{5.30}$$

$$y_-^l \geq 0, \qquad \text{for all } l \in \Omega, \tag{5.31}$$

$$\sum_{i=1}^{n} P_{0i} x_i = V_0, \tag{5.32}$$

$$x \in X. \tag{5.33}$$

We observe that if we set $\omega = 0$, Model PFO-5.4.3 is equivalent to the tracking model Model PFO-5.3.5, and the ε-regret models generalize tracking models.

We implement Models PFO-5.4.1 and PFO-5.4.3 in two variants. Namely, we first maximize the expected return, while placing a bound on the expected regret, and then minimize the expected regret while requiring the expected return to be greater than a given target. Of course, both formulations, with and without the ε-regret, will deliver the same efficient frontier. The main equations and statements are displayed here:

```
ExpRegretCon ..        SUM(1, pr(1) * Regrets(1)) =L= RISK_TARGET;
RegretCon(1) ..        Regrets(1) =G= TargetIndex(1) * Budget -
                       SUM(i, P(i,1) * x(i));
EpsRegretCon(1) ..     Regrets(1) =G= (TargetIndex(1) - EpsRegret) *
                       Budget - SUM(i, P(i,1) * x(i));
ObjDefRegret ..        z =E= SUM(1, pr(1) * Regrets(1));
ObjDefReturn ..        z =E= SUM(i, EP(i) * x(i));

MODEL MinRegret /BudgetCon, ReturnCon, RegretCon, ObjDefRegret/;
MODEL MaxReturn /BudgetCon, ExpRegretCon, RegretCon, ObjDefReturn/;
```

To run Model PFO-5.4.3, simply replace `RegretCon` with `EpsRegretCon` in the `MODEL` statements.

In Figure 5.4 we show the efficient frontiers for ε-regret 1%, 2%, and 3%, respectively. By increasing ε-regret the efficient frontier moves upward. This is also observed in Figure 5.1, where the efficient frontier is moved upward by lowering the target return. Indeed, adding the ε-regret tolerance is equivalent to reducing the target return g^l.

We point out that the efficient frontiers displayed in Figure 5.1 and 5.4 are plotted together for convenience. In other words, the efficient frontiers further up in the graph do

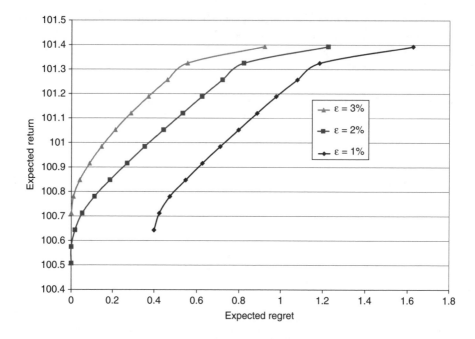

Figure 5.4: ε-regret efficient frontiers obtained with ε equal to 1%, 2%, and 3%. By increasing the ε-regret parameter, the efficient frontier is pushed further up.

not dominate those below, in the usual sense of efficient frontiers, since the portfolios also differ in the target liability (Figure 5.1), or in the maximum allowable regret (Figure 5.4).

5.4.1 The FINLIB files

The GAMS source code and data for the models of this section are given in the following files:

- Regret.gms

5.5 Conditional Value-at-Risk Models

The Value-at-Risk (VaR) concept defined in Section PFO-2.6 can be used to control the risk profile of portfolios and is considered an industry standard. However, VaR minimization leads to integer programming models that are very difficult to solve when the number of scenarios involved is high.

The notion of Conditional Value-at-Risk (CVaR) comes in handy when optimization is required (see Definition PFO-2.6.3). First, CVaR has the nice theoretical property of being a coherent measure as discussed in Section PFO-2.7. Furthermore, CVaR is a convex, smooth function of the portfolio composition, and if the loss function is linear and scenarios are given in discrete form, the CVaR formula is a linear function of the asset allocation, and hence we can optimize this risk measure using linear programming. Finally, since CVaR is always greater than VaR, minimization of CVaR also bounds VaR.

The minimization of Conditional Value-at-Risk (CVaR) is given in Model PFO-5.5.1, which is reproduced here:

Model PFO-5.5.1 Minimization of CVaR

$$\text{Minimize} \quad \zeta + \frac{\sum_{l \in \Omega} p^l y^l_+}{1 - \alpha} \tag{5.34}$$

$$\text{subject to} \quad \sum_{i=1}^{n} \overline{P}_i x_i \geq \mu V_0, \tag{5.35}$$

$$y^l_+ \geq L(x; P^l) - \zeta, \qquad \text{for all } l \in \Omega, \tag{5.36}$$

$$y^l_+ \geq 0, \qquad \text{for all } l \in \Omega, \tag{5.37}$$

$$\sum_{i=1}^{n} P_{0i} x_i = V_0, l \tag{5.38}$$

$$x \in X. \tag{5.39}$$

The constraint structure of the CVaR model is similar to the MAD and regret models. In particular, equation (5.36) has the same form as the regret equation (5.24), and the MAD equations (5.3)–(5.4). Unlike those models, the variable ζ (which is the VaR value) plays the same role of a tolerance or regret, but it is also a variable of the optimization model itself.

Model PFO-5.5.1 is a linear model, provided the loss function $L(x, P^l)$ is a linear function of the portfolio x, which is usually the case. In our setting we use three linear loss functions as follows:

- $L(x; P^l) = V_0 - V(x; P^l)$, loss of the final portfolio value $V(x; P^l)$, with respect to the initial investment V_0.

- $L(x; P^l) = g^l - V(x; P^l)$, loss with respect to a random target g^l (or a fixed target, in case $g^l = g$ for all scenarios $l \in \Omega$). A portfolio model with this loss function is also known as benchmark VaR.

- $L(x; P^l) = V(x; \overline{P}) - V(x; P^l)$, loss with respect to an endogenous target given by the expected value of the portfolio. In this case, if the returns are multivariate normal, the CVaR portfolio and the mean-variance portfolio will coincide; see Uryasev and Rockafellar (2000).

The linearity of the risk measure makes the CVaR model suitable for an alternative formulation, as was also done in the regret and the MAD models, whereby we maximize the expected return of the portfolio and restrict the level of the CVaR to be less or equal to a target risk ω. We reproduce the model with CVaR constraints in Model PFO-5.5.2.

Model PFO-5.5.2 Portfolio optimization with CVaR constraints

$$\text{Maximize} \quad \sum_{i=1}^{n} \overline{P}_i x_i \tag{5.40}$$

$$\text{subject to} \quad \zeta + \frac{\sum_{l \in \Omega} p^l y_+^l}{1 - \alpha} \leq \omega, \tag{5.41}$$

$$y_+^l \geq L(x; P^l) - \zeta, \qquad \text{for all } l \in \Omega, \tag{5.42}$$

$$y_+^l \geq 0, \qquad \text{for all } l \in \Omega, \tag{5.43}$$

$$\sum_{i=1}^{n} P_{0i} x_i = V_0, \tag{5.44}$$

$$x \in X. \tag{5.45}$$

The GAMS code for both Models PFO-5.5.1 and PFO-5.5.2 can be found in `CVaR.gms`. The implementation uses the same approach adopted for the regret models, namely, we declared two equations that will compute, respectively, the CVaR and the expected return of the portfolio:

```
ObjDefCVaR ..  z =E= Var + SUM(l, pr(l) * VaRDev(l)) / (1 - alpha);
ObjDefReturn .. z =E= SUM(i, EP(i) * x(i));
```

Using the dollar statement we declare in a single equation the three different loss functions, and the parameter `LossFlag` will switch to the desired definition.

```
LossDef(l)..
  Losses(l) =E= (Budget - SUM(i, P(i,l) * x(i)))$(LossFlag = 1) +
  (TargetIndex(l) * Budget - SUM(i, P(i,l) * x(i)))$(LossFlag = 2) +
  (SUM(i, EP(i) * x(i)) - SUM(i, P(i,l) * x(i)))$(LossFlag = 3);
```

Finally, `CVaRCon` and `VaRDevCon(l)` describe the CVaR constraints and the deviations from `VaR` for every scenario:

```
CVaRCon .. Var + SUM(l, pr(l) * VaRDev(l)) / (1 - alpha)
           =L= RISK_TARGET;
VaRDevCon(l) .. VaRDev(l) =G= Losses(l) - VaR;
```

In Figure 5.5 we show the mean-CVaR efficient frontiers for different values of the confidence level α. Since a higher α implies that we are interested in more extreme losses, for the same level of the target return the expected CVaR is higher, and therefore the efficient frontiers are squeezed together toward the bottom.

5.5.1 The FINLIB files

The GAMS source code and data for the models of this section are given in the following files:

- `CVaR.gms`

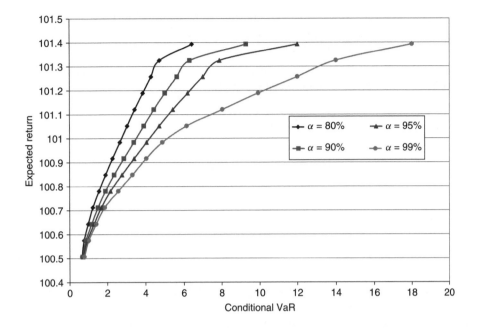

Figure 5.5: CVaR efficient frontiers obtained by varying α. As α increases (80%, 90%, 95%, 99%), the efficient frontiers are pushed downwards, since for the same level of expected return a higher VaR of the losses distribution has to be selected.

5.6   Utility Maximization Models

Utility theory provides a theoretical framework for optimizing investor behavior when faced with uncertainty. The basic assumption in utility theory is that decision makers act, or should act, to maximize their expected utility and we implement models to do so based on Section PFO-5.6.

Letting $\tilde{R}_p$ denote the stochastic return of a portfolio, and R_p^l the return under scenario l in a scenario-based model, then the objective to maximize expected utility is:

$$\text{Max } \mathcal{E}[\mathcal{U}(\tilde{R}_p)] = \sum_{l \in \Omega} p^l \mathcal{U}(R_p^l)$$

where $\mathcal{U}(\cdot)$ is the utility function. The utility function must be monotonically increasing; a concave utility function is consistent with risk-averse behavior, while a convex utility function is consistent with risk-seeking behavior. A linear utility function implies risk-neutral behavior.

A class of utility functions often used in financial optimization are the isoelastic utility functions (Definition PFO-2.8.6), a special case of which is the growth optimal utility function (Definition PFO-2.8.7). They are parameterized by a risk parameter $\gamma \leq 1$, whereby lower gamma values imply higher risk aversion, while $\gamma = 1$ denotes risk neutrality:

$$\mathcal{U}_\gamma(r) = \begin{cases} \frac{1}{\gamma}(1+r)^\gamma & \text{for } \gamma \neq 0, \\ \log(1+r) & \text{for } \gamma = 0. \end{cases} \tag{5.46}$$

The formal connection between the two branches of definition (5.46) is that the expression $\frac{1}{\gamma}((1+r)^{\gamma} - 1)$ converges (pointwise) to $\log(1+r)$ for $\gamma \to 0$.

We repeat here Model PFO-5.6.1 to maximize the expected utility:

Model PFO-5.6.1 Expected utility maximization

$$\text{Maximize} \quad \sum_{l \in \Omega} p^l \mathcal{U}(R(x; r^l)) \tag{5.47}$$

$$\text{subject to} \quad R(x; r^l) = \sum_{i=1}^{n} r_i^l x_i, \tag{5.48}$$

$$\sum_{i=1}^{n} x_i = 1, \tag{5.49}$$

$$x \in X. \tag{5.50}$$

In Utility.gms we implement a slightly different version of Model PFO-5.6.1 which is consistent with the problem discussed in the application on insurance policies with guarantees (see Chapter PFO-12 and Section 8.4 later in this book). The model we implement is more general than Model PFO-5.6.1; in particular we assume that the decision maker has to allocate a given amount of equity among the available assets in order to maximize the expected utility of the return on equity (ROE). The ROE is given by the ratio between the final wealth provided by the portfolio and the initial equity invested:

$$\text{ROE}^l(x, P^l) = \frac{V(x, P^l)}{E}. \tag{5.51}$$

We declare in GAMS the variables ROE(1) and use them as arguments of the utility function. (This is not really necessary, and the dimension of the model can be reduced by substituting the definition of the ROE directly in the objective function. However, readability is improved with the use of dummy variables.) To handle the case for $\gamma = 0$, we split ObjDef in two parts using the dollar statement:

```
POSITIVE VARIABLES
    ROE(1)   Return on Equity ;

EquityCon ..   SUM(i, x(i))  =E= Equity;
ROEDef(1)..    ROE(1)        =E= SUM(i, P(i,1) * x(i)) / Equity;
ObjDef ..      z =E= SUM(1,pr(1)
                  * ((1.0/gamma * ROE(1)**gamma) $(gamma <> 0) +
                     LOG(ROE(1))                  $(gamma = 0))));

MODEL ExpectedUtility /EquityCon, ROEDef, ObjDef/;
```

We solve ExpectedUtility for a sequence of risk aversion parameter, gamma, compute the certainty equivalent ROE CeROE, and store the correspondent portfolios in a file.

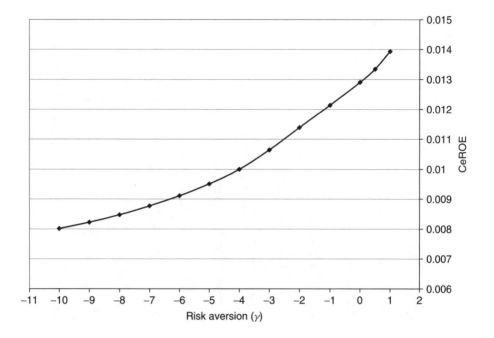

Figure 5.6: Risk aversion vs CeROE; the higher the risk aversion (i.e., large negative values of γ) the lower the CeROE.

In Figure 5.6, we show the CeROE as a function of the risk aversion parameter gamma. As expected, the lower the gamma the higher the risk aversion, and therefore the lower the CeROE achieved. This occurs because risk-averse investors will prefer to allocate their equity on less risky assets. The latter, in general, have a lower expected return, thus lowering the final performance of the portfolio. In Figure 5.7, we display the portfolios obtained for different values of gamma. The risk-neutral investor (gamma $=$ 1) will allocate the whole Equity on a single asset, while the risk-averse investors will diversify their investment among the available assets.

5.6.1   The FINLIB files

The GAMS source code and data for the models of this section are given in the following files:

- Utility.gms

5.7   Put/Call Efficient Frontier Models

Put/call models are analyzed in Section PFO-5.7.1. They provide a framework to select portfolios whose risk measure is given by the expected value of the downside deviations from a given target, and the reward measure is the expected value of the upside deviations

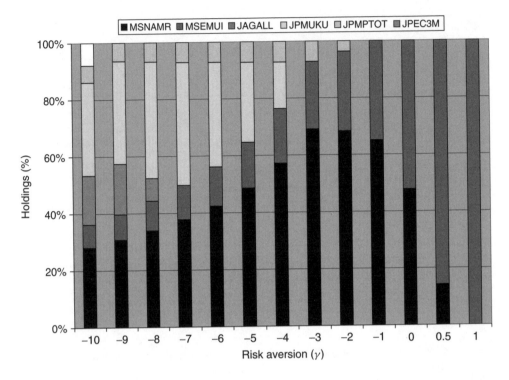

Figure 5.7: Asset allocation for different levels of risk aversion. For higher risk aversion (i.e., large negative values of γ) the asset allocation is more diversified.

from the same target. Put/call models also provide a valuable tool to determine the liquidity premium or discount with respect to prices under infinite liquidity.

We replicate here Model PFO-5.7.1 that generates unconstrained efficient put/call portfolios:

Model PFO-5.7.1 Put/call efficient portfolio

$$\text{Maximize} \quad \sum_{l \in \Omega} p^l y_+^l \tag{5.52}$$

$$\text{subject to} \quad \sum_{l \in \Omega} p^l y_-^l \leq \omega, \tag{5.53}$$

$$y_+^l - y_-^l - \sum_{i=1}^{n} (P_i^l - P_{0i} I^l) x_i = 0, \quad \text{for all } l \in \Omega, \tag{5.54}$$

$$y_+^l, y_-^l \geq 0, \quad \text{for all } l \in \Omega. \tag{5.55}$$

Note that Model PFO-5.7.1 is unconstrained and its dual formulation is given below:

Model PFO-5.7.2 Dual put/call efficient portfolio

$$\text{Minimize }\ \omega\pi_\omega \tag{5.56}$$

$$\text{subject to }\ \sum_{l\in\Omega}(P_i^l - P_{0i}I^l)\pi^l = 0, \qquad \text{for all } i \in U, \tag{5.57}$$

$$p^l\pi_\omega - \pi^l \geq 0, \qquad \text{for all } l \in \Omega, \tag{5.58}$$

$$\pi^l \geq p^l, \qquad \text{for all } l \in \Omega, \tag{5.59}$$

$$\pi_\omega \geq 0. \tag{5.60}$$

The solution of Model PFO-5.7.1 yields the dual prices π^l, and those, when normalized, contribute to determining the infinite liquidity benchmark-neutral price of the securities $i \in U$ (see Section PFO-5.7.1 and in particular Equation PFO-5.147).

In the file `PutCall.gms` we implement both the primal Model PFO-5.7.1 and its dual, Model PFO-5.7.2.

The equations that define both models are given here:

```
% Primal equations

PutCon  ..             SUM(l, pr(l) * yNeg(l) ) =L= Omega;
TargetDevDef(l) ..     SUM(i, ( P(i,l) - TargetIndex(l) ) * x(i) ) =E=
                       yPos(l) -  yNeg(l);
ObjDef      ..         z =E= SUM(l, pr(l) * yPos(l));


% Dual equations
DualObjDef ..          z =E= Omega * PiOmega;
DualTrackingDef(i)..   SUM(l, (P(i,l) - TargetIndex(l))
                       * Pi(l)) =E= 0.0;
MeasureDef(l)..        pr(l) * PiOmega - Pi(l) =G= 0;


Pi.LO(l) = pr(l);
```

Note that constraints $\pi^l \geq p^l$ are defined using the lower bound attribute `Pi.LO(1)` = `pr(1)`.

Of course, we know from linear programming theory (see Appendix PFO-A) that it is not necessary to write explicitly the dual problem. The optimal values of the dual variables are immediately at hand with the GAMS linear programming solver by using the attribute `M` for variables and equations. For instance, π^l are the dual prices for (5.54), and π_ω is the dual price for (5.53). They are both displayed with:

```
DISPLAY TargetDevDef.M, PutCon.M;
```

The reader can simply check that the values in `TargetDevDef.M` coincide with the `Pi.L`, and `PutCon.M` coincides with `PiOmega.L`, where `Pi.L` and `PiOmega.L` are the variables of the dual Model PFO-5.7.2.

In case the put/call model is unconstrained, the dual price `PutCon.M` is constant for different levels of the coefficient ω. By adding liquidity constraints – for example, by setting upper and lower bounds on the amounts held for each security – the dual price `PutCon.M` is a stepwise decreasing function of the coefficient ω, and the efficient frontier is a concave function of ω.

Model PFO-5.7.3 with liquidity constraints is reproduced here:

Model PFO-5.7.3 Put/call efficient portfolio with finite liquidity

---

$$\text{Maximize} \quad \sum_{l \in \Omega} p^l y^l_+ \tag{5.61}$$

$$\text{subject to} \quad \sum_{l \in \Omega} p^l y^l_- \le \omega, \tag{5.62}$$

$$y^l_+ - y^l_- - \sum_{i=1}^{n} (P^l_i - P_{0i} I^l) x_i = 0, \qquad \text{for all } l \in \Omega, \tag{5.63}$$

$$-x_i \le -\underline{x}_i, \qquad \text{for all } i \in U, \tag{5.64}$$

$$x_i \le \overline{x}_i, \qquad \text{for all } i \in U, \tag{5.65}$$

$$y^l_+, y^l_- \ge 0, \qquad \text{for all } l \in \Omega. \tag{5.66}$$

We implement this model simply by setting the upper and lower bounds for each asset $i \in U$. We then collect the dual prices from `TargetDevDef.M(l)` and `x.M(i)`. Note that the dual prices have to be taken with the opposite sign to correctly compute liquidity premium and discount.

We run Model PFO-5.7.3 with a mild and a tight set of liquidity constraints. These are given as:

```
* Mild liquidity constraints
x.LO(i)  = -100.0;
x.UP(i)  = 100.0;

* Tight liquidity constraints
x.LO(i)  = -20.0;
x.UP(i)  = 20.0;
```

We show in Figure 5.8 the dual price π_ω for different risk levels ω. The model with mild liquidity constraints yields the curve with higher dual prices, and this is more pronounced when ω is small. In fact, to satisfy the put constraint when ω is small implies a strong trading (short or long) in the most attractive securities. When the model has tighter liquidity constraints, the gain in relaxing ω is less pronounced, since trading is already limited.

Liquidity constraints also have an influence on the put/call efficient frontiers. A tight bound on the trading activity will force the use of those securities that have the highest upside for a given downside. The trade-off rate between the call value and the put value is thus reduced, and the efficient frontier becomes more concave (see Figure 5.9).

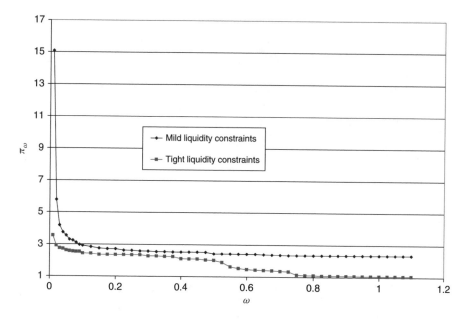

Figure 5.8: Dual price π_ω for different risk levels ω. The two curves are drawn using two different sets of liquidity constraints. The model with less liquidity (tight constraints) yields lower dual prices as the trading activity is already bounded in a small range of values, and by relaxing ω the objective function improves only slightly.

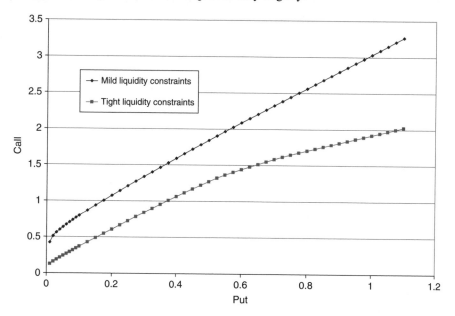

Figure 5.9: Put/call efficient frontiers using two different sets of liquidity constraints. The tighter the liquidity constraints, the more concave the efficient frontier, which is dominated by efficient frontiers with mild constraints on liquidity.

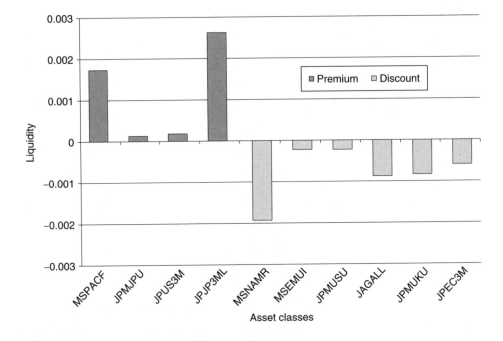

Figure 5.10: Liquidity premia and discounts for risk level $\omega = 0.475$. Securities trading at their upper bounds yield a discount premium. By relaxing the upper bounds for such securities, the expected upside will increase; therefore, a discount is received to trade at the given bound.

Finally, we determine the liquidity premia for a given risk level ω. As explained in Section PFO-5.7.1, the presence of upper and lower bounds on the amount held for each security generates liquidity cost. Model PFO-5.7.3 allows the estimate of such costs. In particular, if a security trades at the lower bound, the associated dual price will be greater than zero, and the liquidity premium is given by $\frac{\pi_i}{\sum_{l \in \Omega} \pi^l I^l}$ where, $\underline{\pi}_i$ is the dual price linked with the lower bound constraint, and π^l are the dual prices linked with the equation defining the deviations from the benchmark. Note that we did not explicitly write the bound constraints, since GAMS sets box constraints through the LO and UP variable attributes. We obtained the dual prices using the attribute M. The GAMS variable extension x.M(i) holds the dual prices $\underline{\pi}_i$, which are negative for securities trading at their lower bound, and $\overline{\pi}_i$, which are positive for securities trading at their upper bound.

The GAMS code to compute the liquidity Premium(i) and Discount(i) is given below:

```
Df = SUM(1, -TargetDevDef.M(1) );
Psi(1) = -TargetDevDef.M(1) / Df;
BenchMarkNeutralPrice(i) = SUM(1, Psi(1) * P(i,1)) /
                           SUM(1, Psi(1) * TargetIndex(1));
Discount(i)(x.M(i) > 0) =  x.M(i) / SUM(1, (-TargetDevDef.M(1))
                           * TargetIndex(1));
```

```
Premium(i)(x.M(i) < 0) =   (-x.M(i)) / SUM(1, (-TargetDevDef.M(1))
                         * TargetIndex(1));
Price(i) = BenchMarkNeutralPrice(i) + Premium(i)   -   Discount(i)
```

The term `Price(i)` carries the current asset prices (P_{0i}). Note that, from the properties of linear programming for dual variables, `Premium(i)` and `Discount(i)` can both be zero – if the security trades in between its bounds – but they cannot both be different than zero. `Price(i)` is thus given by the `BenchMarkNeutralPrice(i)` plus `Premium(i)` and minus `Discount(i)`. Since we built the model such that the initial prices are all equal to one, we also expect that `Price(i)` is equal to one.

In Figure 5.10 we display the liquidity premium and discount for each asset. The security labeled MSPACF is traded at its lower bound; this means that we have to pay a premium to keep it in our portfolio. If no lower bound was set for MSPACF, the optimal solution will short as much as possible of this asset, thus improving the objective function. The opposite occurs for MSNAMR that is traded at its upper bound, and therefore yields a liquidity discount.

5.7.1   The FINLIB files

The GAMS source code and data for the models of this section are given in the following file:

- `PutCall.gms`

Chapter 6

Dynamic Portfolio Optimization with Stochastic Programming

6.1 Preview

In this chapter we develop the GAMS models for dynamic portfolio optimization using stochastic programming. The development is based on the discussion of Chapter PFO-6. The following models are discussed in this chapter and the GAMS source code for each is given in the associated FINLIB files:

Stochastic dedication models are based on Section PFO-6.4, and combine the static fixed-income portfolio models with scenario optimization. These models are stochastic extensions of the fixed-income models discussed in Chapter 4.

- StochDedication.gms
- StochDedicationBL.gms

Two-stage and multi-stage stochastic programs are based on Sections PFO-6.5 and PFO-6.6, and extend the scenario models analyzed in Chapter 5 to allow dynamic rebalancing of portfolios as time evolves and new information becomes known.

- TwoStageDeterministic.gms
- TwoStageStochastic.gms
- ThreeStageSPDA.gms

6.2 Dynamic Optimization for Fixed-Income Securities

As a first step towards building stochastic programming models for portfolio optimization we extend the immunization and dedication models from Sections 4.3 and 4.4 to incorporate scenarios. All the models here are built upon the finite scenario set Ω, indexed by l.

6.2.1   Stochastic dedication

We start with Model PFO-6.4.1. This is a stochastic dedication model with an objective function and risk constraints, as given in the put/call framework of Section PFO-5.7.
    The model is given below:

Model PFO-6.4.1 Put/call efficient frontier for stochastic dedication

---

$$\text{Maximize} \quad \sum_{l \in \Omega} p^l y_+^l \tag{6.1}$$

$$\text{subject to} \quad \sum_{i=1}^{n} P_{0i} x_{0i} \leq v_0, \tag{6.2}$$

$$\sum_{l \in \Omega} p^l y_-^l \leq \omega, \tag{6.3}$$

$$y_+^l - y_-^l - \sum_{i=1}^{n} P_{0i}^l x_{0i} = P_L^l, \qquad \text{for all } l \in \Omega, \tag{6.4}$$

$$y_+, y_- \geq 0. \tag{6.5}$$

The model assumes that spot rates in the future are uncertain, hence, the present values of bonds as well as the liabilities are uncertain and indexed by scenario l. The model makes no assumptions on the nature of the process that generates future spot rates, and to highlight the connection to the immunization models of Sections 4.4 and 4.5, we will use the interest-rate factors given there to generate scenarios. In particular, we assume that each scenario is constructed by perturbing the short rates by some fraction of each factor. This is given in GAMS by the following code fragment:

```
PARAMETER
   Sr(t,l)                  Spot rate scenarios;


PARAMETER
   FactorWeights(j,l)   Weights of each factor under each scenario
   /FF_1.SS_1  0.01,  FF_1.SS_2 -0.02, FF_1.SS_3 0.04,
   FF_2.SS_4  0.02,  FF_2.SS_5  0.01, FF_2.SS_6 0.01,
   FF_3.SS_7 -0.01,  FF_3.SS_8 -0.01, FF_3.SS_9 -0.02/;


Sr(t,l)$(r(t) <> 0) = r(t) + SUM(j, FactorWeights(j, l) * beta(j,t));
```

The parameter `FactorWeights` shows the weight of each factor in perturbing the basic spot rates, and is used to calculate the uncertain future spot rates `Sr`. Recall that `beta(j,t)` are the factor loadings (Definition PFO-2.4.14), where j denotes factors and t denotes time (see `FactorData.inc`). The scenario probabilities are specified by:

```
PARAMETERS
   pr(l)                 Scenario probability
```

```
/SS_1 = 10, SS_2 = 5, SS_3 = 11,
 SS_4 = 2,  SS_5 = 7, SS_6 = 9,
 SS_7 = 15, SS_8 = 3, SS_9 = 3/;
```

```
* Scale probabilities to one.
```

```
pr(l) = pr(l) / SUM(ll, pr(ll));
```

Here, each scenario is first given a weight, and then the probabilities are scaled to add up to one. This code segment illustrates the use of GAMS as a simulator. Of course, this scenario set may or may not make sense for a particular application. In general, scenarios are generated outside the portfolio optimization model; see Chapter PFO-9.

The next step is to calculate the present values of both sides of the balance sheet. These are scenario dependent and are computed as follows:

```
PARAMETERS
    P(i)      Implied market price
    PV(i,l)   Bonds present value
    PVL(l)    Liabilities present value;
```

```
PV(i,l) = SUM(t, F(t,i) * EXP(-Sr(t,l) * tau(t)));
PVL(l)  = SUM(t, Liability(t) * exp(-Sr(t,l) * tau(t)));
P(i)    = SUM(l, pr(l) * PV(i,l) );
```

Also recall that the price of each bond is given as the expected value over all scenarios with zero-option adjusted spread (see Definition PFO-2.4.15). In contrast with Section PFO-6.4, we use continuous discounting in our implementation, consistent with the other GAMS models implemented in this book.

The rest of the model is now quite straightforward. The key concept is to extend the scenario-dependent variables and constraints of the immunization model (Immunization.gms) from Section 4.4 by a scenario index, l:

```
SCALARS
    Budget  Initial budget /800000/
    Omega   Bound on the expected shortfalls /1275/;
```

```
POSITIVE VARIABLES
    yPos(l)      Positive deviations
    yNeg(l)      Negative deviations
    x(i)         Holdings of assets in monetary units
                 (not proportions);
```

```
VARIABLE
    z            Objective function value;
```

```
EQUATIONS
    BudgetCon         Equation defining the budget constraint
    ObjDef            Objective function definition for MAD
```

```
     TargetDevDef(l)         Equations defining the positive
                             and negative deviations
     PutCon                  Constraint to bound the expected value
                             of the negative deviations ;

ObjDef ..                    z =E= SUM(l, pr(l) * yPos(l));

BudgetCon ..                 SUM(i, P(i) * x(i)) =E= Budget;

PutCon ..                    SUM(l, pr(l) * yNeg(l)) =L= Omega;

TargetDevDef(l) ..           SUM(i, PV(i,l) * x(i)) =E= PVL(l) +
                             yPos(l) - yNeg(l);
```

Note that for some indices l, it may happen that both `yPos(l)` and `yNeg(l)` are non-zero. This occurs because the model will find first a feasible solution, and then, if the `PutCon` constraint is not tight, it will increase a pair of `yPos(l)` and `yNeg(l)` variables to improve the objective.

The model in this case is exploiting the fully allowable downside risk given by `Omega` to top up the upside. Constraints of the form `yPos(l) * yNeg(l) =E= 0` can be added to ensure that only one of the variables is non-zero, but this gives rise to a nonlinearly constrained model, which might be difficult to solve. Furthermore, since we are interested in building efficient frontiers with the smallest downside risk, we usually set ω to small values such that `PutCon` is active, thus avoiding the need to add nonlinear constraints. In any event, the investment decision given by `x(i)` will be correct, so the problem with the increase in the y variables does not pose a significant practical problem.

Alternatively, we can cast the objective function to maximize the expected upside and minimize the expected downside, by penalizing the latter by a weight `lambda`, strictly greater than one:

```
ObjDef .. z =E= SUM(l, pr(l) * yPos(l)) -
                lambda * SUM(l, pr(l) * yNeg(l)).
```

The reader may wish to implement a model with such an objective function and check that both `yPos(l)` and `yNeg(l)` will be non-zero.

6.2.2   Stochastic dedication with borrowing and lending

In contrast to the stochastic dedication model, the dedication model with borrowing and lending, Model PFO-6.4.2, assumes that future cashflows and liabilities are inherently stochastic and depend on the state of the economy denoted by s for a set Σ_t of plausible states at period t. The uncertainty of interest rates in this case may not be the only source of uncertainty as was the assumption in stochastic dedication.

Model PFO-6.4.2 Stochastic dedication

$$\text{Minimize} \quad v_0 \tag{6.6}$$

$$\text{subject to} \qquad \sum_{i=1}^{n} F_{0i} x_{0i} + v_0 + v_0^{-0} = L_0^0 + v_0^{+0}, \tag{6.7}$$

$$\sum_{i=1}^{n} F^s_{(t-1)i} x_{0i} + (1 + r^s_{f(t-1)}) v_{t-1}^{+s^-} + v_t^{-s} = L_t^s + v_t^{+s} \tag{6.8}$$

$$+ (1 + r^s_{f(t-1)} + \delta) v_{t-1}^{-s^-},$$

$$\text{for all } t \in \mathcal{T}, \ s \in \Sigma_t,$$

$$x, v^+, v^- \geq 0. \tag{6.9}$$

The implementation of this model is given in StochDedicationBL.gms. We first generate random data as follows:

```
SF(t,i,1) = F(t,i) * UNIFORM(0.6, 2.0);
SFactorWeights('FF_1',1)=  FactorWeights('FF_1',1) *
    UNIFORM(0.8,1.4);
SFactorWeights('FF_2',1) = FactorWeights('FF_2',1) *
    UNIFORM(0.9,1.1);
SFactorWeights('FF_3',1) = FactorWeights('FF_3',1) *
    UNIFORM(0.95,1.05);

SLiability(t,1) = Liability(t) * UNIFORM(0.8, 1.4);

Srf(t,1) = rf(t) * UNIFORM(0.8, 1.2);

Sr(t,1)$(r(t) <> 0) = r(t) + SUM(j,SFactorWeights(j,1)*beta(j,t));

SF('2001','i',1) = SUM(t, SF(t,i,1) * EXP (- Sr(t,1) * tau(t)) );

* Implied market price

Price(i) = ( 1.0 / CARD(1) ) * SUM(1, SF('2001',i,1) );
```

The stochastic parameters are SF (scenarios of cashflows corresponding to F^s_{ti} in the model), SLiability (scenarios of liabilities corresponding to L_t^s), SFactorWeights (scenarios of factor weights used to generate the spot rates), Sr (scenarios of spot rates to compute the bond prices under each scenario), and Srf, the stochastic future period-by-period reinvestment yield, corresponding to r^s_{ft}. The implied bond prices are given by the expected value of the present values of each cashflow. Note that such quantities enter in the model as F_{0i}, and since they represent a cost, their sign must be negated.

In realistic applications the generation of these stochastic data would require the use of suitable scenario generation methods; see Chapter PFO-9. Given scenario data, the model is now a simple extension of the dedication model of Section 4.3:

```
POSITIVE VARIABLES
    x(i)                Face value purchased
    surplus(t,l)        Amount of money reinvested
    borrow(t,l)         Amount of money borrowed;


VARIABLE
    v0                      Upfront investment;

CashFlowCon(t,l) ..    SUM(i, SF(t,i,l) * x(i))    $ (tau(t) > 0) +
    ( v0 - SUM(i, Price(i) * x(i)) )               $ (tau(t) = 0) +
    ( (1 + Srf(t-1,l)) * surplus(t-1,l) )          $ (tau(t) > 0) +
    borrow(t,l)                                    $ (tau(t) < Horizon)
    =E= surplus(t,l) + SLiability(t,l)             $ (tau(t) > 0) +
    (( 1 + Srf(t-1,l) + spread ) * borrow(t-1,l))  $ (tau(t) > 0);

MODEL StochDedicationBL /CashFlowCon/;

SOLVE StochDedicationBL MINIMIZING v0 USING LP;
```

6.2.3   The FINLIB files

The GAMS source code and data for the models of this section are given in the following files:

- StochDedication.gms

- StochDedicationBL.gms

- BondData.inc

- FactorData.inc

- SpotRates.inc

6.3   Formulating Two-Stage Stochastic Programs

There are different ways to formulate stochastic models algebraically and then to implement them in GAMS. In this section, we develop a simple two-stage portfolio management problem using the so called "compact" formulation which is, as the name suggests, the most economical in terms of number of variables and constraints. Other formulations are possible, but their usefulness depends on the availability of algorithms that can exploit the algebraic structure obtained by reformulating the problem. General purpose solvers provide some options to take advantage of the model structure, but specialized solvers are needed to obtain superior performances. Just as an example, we will formulate a "split variable" model in Section 6.4, but no specific algorithms will be implemented to take advantage of the algebraic structure obtained. The interested reader can turn to PFO or to Censor and Zenios (1997) for relevant references on this issue. The general stochastic programming formulation for the portfolio optimization models implemented here is covered in Chapter PFO-6 and, in particular, Sections PFO-6.5 and PFO-6.6.

6.3.1   Deterministic and stochastic two-stage programs

We consider an investor with a budget of 10,000€ to invest over a one-year horizon. The investment can be readjusted after six months, but no new money is injected. The objective is to maximize the expected terminal value of the final portfolio, subject to the constraint that under no circumstances must the final value be less than 11,500€. There are three assets available for the initial (first-stage) investment: a stock, and a put and a call option on this stock. Similarly, there are three assets available for investing during the second stage: the same stock, and two new options, again a put and a call. All the options have maturities of six months.

In general we have:

- U_1 and U_2, the sets of assets available in stages 1 and 2.

- V_j, the final (horizon) value of asset $j \in A_2$.

- P_{1j} and P_{2k}, the asset prices at the beginning of stages 1 and 2, for each $j \in U_1$ and $k \in U_2$.

- x_j, first-stage holdings for each asset $j \in U_1$.

- y_k, second-stage holdings for each asset $k \in U_2$.

At first we assume, unrealistically of course, that the future is completely known, so that we know the prices and values of all assets into the future. This results in the following deterministic dynamic problem:

$$\underset{x,y}{\text{Maximize}} \sum_{k \in U_2} V_k y_k \tag{6.10}$$

$$\text{subject to} \sum_{j \in U_1} P_{1j} x_j \leq v_0, \tag{6.11}$$

$$\sum_{k \in U_2} V_k y_k \geq \mu, \tag{6.12}$$

$$\sum_{j \in U_1} P_{2j} x_j \geq \sum_{k \in U_2} V_k y_k, \tag{6.13}$$

$$x_j \geq 0, \qquad \text{for all } j \in U_1, \tag{6.14}$$

$$y_k \geq 0, \qquad \text{for all } k \in U_2. \tag{6.15}$$

Equations (6.11) and (6.12) are, respectively, the budget and the minimum return constraint. Equation (6.13) ensures that the final value of the first-stage portfolio is not less than the initial value of the second-stage portfolio, i.e., it is a rebalancing constraint.

The GAMS formulation for (6.10)–(6.15) quite straightforward:

```
SET Assets Available asset
   /Stock, Put_1, Call_1, Put_2, Call_2/;

SET Assets_1(Assets) Assets available up to the end of the
     first stage
   /Stock, Put_1, Call_1/;

SET Assets_2(Assets) Assets available up to the end of the
     second stage
   /Stock, Put_2, Call_2/;

ALIAS (Assets, i );
ALIAS (Assets_1, j);
ALIAS (Assets_2, k);

POSITIVE VARIABLES
   x(j)      First-stage (or first-stage) holdings
   y(k)      Second-stage (or second-stage) holdings;

VARIABLE
   z         Objective function value;

EQUATIONS
   BudgetCon           Equation defining the budget constraint
   ObjDef              Objective function definition
   MinReturnCon        Equation defining the minimum return constraint
   RebalanceCon        Equation defining the rebalancing constraint;

ObjDef ..        z =E= SUM(k, V(k) * y(k));
BudgetCon ..     SUM(j, P_1(j) *x(j))    =L= 10000;
MinReturnCon ..  SUM(k, V(k) * y(k))     =G= 11500;
RebalanceCon ..  SUM(j, P_2(j) * x(j))   =G= SUM(k, P_2(k) *
                    y(k));

MODEL DeterministicTwoStage 'PFO Model 6.4.2' /ALL/;
SOLVE DeterministicTwoStage MAXIMIZING z USING LP;
```

The optimal objective value of this problem is 429,414€, which is obviously an unrealistic return from an initial budget of 10,000€. The problem of course is that in the absence of return uncertainty, the put options in both stages are wonderful investments – too good to be true.

We introduce uncertainty into the problem using three scenarios for returns. The initial prices of the stock and the first-stage options are known, but their values at the end of the first, and at the end of the second stage, are stochastic – they differ for each of the three scenarios.

The formal stochastic model for this problem is now:

$$\text{Maximize}_{x,y} \sum_{l \in \Omega} p^l \sum_{k \in U_2} V_k^l y_k^l \tag{6.16}$$

$$\text{subject to} \sum_{j \in U_1} P_{1j} x_j \leq v_0, \tag{6.17}$$

$$\sum_{k \in U_2} V_k^l y_k^l \geq \mu, \qquad \text{for all } l \in \Omega, \tag{6.18}$$

$$\sum_{j \in U_1} P_{2j}^l x_j \geq \sum_{k \in U_2} V_k^l y_k^l, \qquad \text{for all } l \in \Omega, \tag{6.19}$$

$$x_j \geq 0, \qquad \text{for all } j \in U_1, \tag{6.20}$$

$$y_k \geq 0, \qquad \text{for all } k \in U_2. \tag{6.21}$$

We have simply equipped all stochastic data, and the second-stage variables y_j^l, with a scenario index $l \in \Omega$, and also use the scenario probabilities p^l, when maximizing the expected horizon value. The changes to the GAMS formulation follow those of the formal model directly. The scenario and data declarations now read:

```
PARAMETER pr(l) Scenario probability
   /SS_1 = 0.25,
    SS_2 = 0.50,
    SS_3 = 0.25/;


PARAMETER P_1(j) Asset prices at the beginning of the first stage
   /Stock = 43,
    Put_1  = 0.81,
    Call_1 = 4.76/;

TABLE P_2(l,i) Asset prices (values) at the beginning of the
   second-stage
            Stock   Put_1  Call_1   Put_2    Call_2
   SS_1     44       1      0        0.92     4.43
   SS_2     36       0      4        1.40     0.85
   SS_3     47       2      0        3.02     6.82;


TABLE V(l,k)  Asset prices (values) at the end of the second stage
            Stock   Put_2      Call_2
   SS_1     48       1          0
   SS_2     32       0          3
   SS_3     55       4          0;


ObjDef ..          z =E= SUM((k,l), pr(l) * V(l,k) * y(l,k));
BudgetCon ..       SUM(j, P_1(j) * x(j))    =L= 10000;
MinReturnCon(l) .. SUM(k, V(l,k) * y(l,k)) =G= 11500;
```

```
RebalanceCon(1)  .. SUM(j, P_2(1,j) * x(j)) =G=
                    SUM(k, P_2(1,k) * y(1,k));

MODEL StochasticTwoStage /ALL/;

SOLVE StochasticTwoStage MAXIMIZING z USING LP;
```

By introducing scenarios for the second stage variables, the portfolio is now more diversified. In particular, we have holdings in `Stock` $= 198.539$ and in `Put`$\backslash_1 = 1805.933$. The expected final value of the selected portfolio is 19,773.925€.

The reader will note that equations (6.16)–(6.21) provide a general framework that can be used to extend the models developed in the previous chapter (MAD, regret minimization, expected utility maximization, etc.).

6.3.2 The FINLIB files

The GAMS source code and data for the models of this section are given in the following files:

- `TwoStageDeterministic.gms`

- `TwoStageStochastic.gms`

6.4 Single Premium Deferred Annuities: A Multi-stage Stochastic Program

We now develop a simple, yet complete, three-stage stochastic program. The resulting model is solved using various objectives, such as maximizing expected returns, maximizing the worst-case outcome, and maximizing expected utility. The GAMS code is explained along the way and the complete model is found in `ThreeStageSPDA.gms`.

6.4.1 Background and data

The setting for the case is an insurance company that manages retirement accounts of various types. One of their products is Single Premium Deferred Annuities, SPDA, (see Section PFO-8.3.3), where the insured (annuitant) pays a lump sum (single premium) into a managed account. The insurance company provides interest payments into this account according to certain rules (subject to caps, floors, etc.), and agrees to pay out an annual amount of money, based on the account balance, to the annuitant from age $59\frac{1}{2}$ onwards. The precise amounts and payment mechanisms are contractually specified. After a lock-in period (typically up to seven years) the annuitant can withdraw all or part of his account. A typical reason for terminating an account is to move the proceeds into a better paying account elsewhere.

We consider a hypothetical insurance company, which we call Winvest, that has just accepted an SPDA contract with a premium of 100,000,000€. The risk manager of Winvest is asked to invest the premium in such a way that if interest rates increase, the company will be able to pay higher interest into the annuitants' accounts, thus avoiding withdrawals

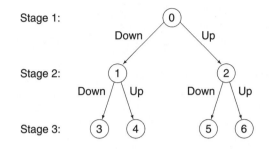

Figure 6.1: Scenario tree for a three-stage program ($T = 3$) having four scenarios. In this example, ξ_2 has three possible realizations, and ξ_3 has two possible realizations for each realization of ξ_2.

(lapse). Recall that the value of a straight bond portfolio decreases when interest rates increase, so straight bonds are not appropriate assets for Winvest. Instead, the company is looking to derivative instruments, in particular mortgage-backed securities (MBSs) on the asset side; see Section PFO-8.3.5 for a discussion of mortgage-backed securities.

The asset and liability sides were both analyzed through interest-rate models. In our simple example model, only short rates were modeled (i.e., we use a one-factor model of the term structure with short rates as the factor) and only two stages are modeled. Today's short rates are known, and for the particular interest-rate model employed the rates during the first stage move either up or down. In the second stage, they again move either up or down, which leads to the event tree, or scenario tree, shown in Figure 6.1, with six states and a total of four scenarios.

The changes in interest rates drive changes in the values on both the asset side (the MBSs) and the liability side (the SPDAs); see Chapter PFO-8.

The basic sets and the data in GAMS format are shown below:

```
SET Scenarios Set of scenarios
   /UU, UD, DD, DU/;

SET Assets  Available assets
   /io2, po7, po70, io90/;

SET Time Time steps
   /t0, t1, t2/;

ALIAS (Scenarios, l); ALIAS (Assets, i); ALIAS (Time, t);

TABLE Yield(i,t,l) Asset yields
                  UU          UD          DD          DU
     IO2 .T0   1.104439    1.104439    0.959238    0.959238
     IO2 .T1   1.110009    0.975907    0.935106    1.167817
     PO7 .T0   0.938159    0.938159    1.166825    1.166825
     PO7 .T1   0.933668    1.154590    1.156536    0.903233
     PO70.T0   0.924840    0.924840    1.167546    1.167546
```

```
        PO70.T1    0.891527    1.200802    1.141917    0.907837
        IO90.T0    1.107461    1.107461    0.908728    0.908728
        IO90.T1    1.105168    0.925925    0.877669    1.187143 ;
```

TABLE CashYield(t,l) Risk-free (cash) yield

	UU	UD	DD	DU
T0	1.030414	1.030414	1.012735	1.012735
T1	1.032623	1.014298	1.009788	1.030481 ;

TABLE Liability(t,l) Liabilities due to annuitant lapses

	UU	UD	DD	DU
T1	26.474340	26.474340	10.953843	10.953843
T2	31.264791	26.044541	10.757200	13.608207 ;

PARAMETER FinalLiability(l)   Final liabilities
    / uu = 47.284751, ud = 49.094838, dd = 86.111238, du = 83.290085/;

The set Scenarios defines the number of total scenarios, consisting of the up-up (denoted by UU in the GAMS model), up-down (UD), down-up (DU) and down-down (DD) sequences. The model uses a small universe of four derivatives of MBSs called IO2, PO7, PO70 and IO90, where IO is a derivative of an MBS that only contains home owners' interest payments, and PO is a derivative of an MBS that only contains their principal payments. The model has only two stages, bounded by the three trading dates T0, T1, and T2.

The table Yield(i,t,l) contains the yields of the MBSs under each scenario, and in each stage. For instance, PO7 drops to 93.3668% of its value during the second stage under the UU scenario, i.e., from stage T1 to stage T2, but it gains 15.4590% under the UD scenario during the same stage. Apart from investing in the mortgage derivatives, one may also invest in cash. The CashYield(t,l) table shows the returns of the risk-free asset. In Liability(t,l), we store the liability payments faced by the insurance company along the way (corresponding to annuitant lapses), while FinalLiability(l) contains the outstanding liabilities originated by the future payments of the annuities to the policyholders.

We model the problem by focusing first on a single scenario. At each of the three trading dates at times T0, T1, and T2, we have the opportunity to buy, sell, or hold amounts of each of the MBSs, or of cash. We introduce the decision variables:

buy(t,i,l), amount to buy of MBS i, at stage t, under scenario l;

sell(t,i,l), amount to sell of MBS i, at stage t, under scenario l;

hold(t,i,l), amount to hold of MBS i, at stage t, under scenario l;

cash(t,l), amount stored in cash at stage t, under scenario l.

It is most convenient to have these variables measure value (not face value amounts) of the investments. Buying and selling securities is essentially conversion from and to cash; we therefore need to keep track of the value invested in each security and in cash, for each scenario. The following MBS balance equations keep track of the MBS holdings:

```
AssetInventoryCon(t,i,l) ..
1           buy(t,i,l)                                  $ (ORD(t) lt CARD(t)) +
2           ( Yield(i,t-1,l) * hold(t-1,i,l) )          $ (ORD(t) gt 1) =E=
3           sell(t,i,l)                                 $ (ORD(t) gt 1) +
4           hold(t,i,l)                                 $ (ORD(t) lt CARD(t));
```

The constraints (one for each stage, for each security, and for each scenario) stipulate that the amount purchased (line 1), plus the amount held from the previous stage (line 2), suitably taking into account the security's yield during that stage, must equal the amount sold (line 3), plus the amount held into the next stage (line 4). The dollar conditions restrict the occurrence of the decision variables. For instance, one can only purchase securities prior to the last stage, and there can be holdings in securities only after the first stage.

We also need to keep track of cash, which is used for two purposes: to store value between stages, and as the intermediate numeraire when buying and selling securities. The cash balance constraints are:

```
CashInventoryCon(t,l) ..
1      SUM(i, sell(t,i,l) * (1 - PropCost)) $ (ORD(t) gt 1) +
2      (CashYield(t-1,l) * cash(t-1,l))         $ (ORD(t) gt 1) +
3      100 $ (ORD(t) eq 1) =E=
4      SUM(i, buy(t,i,l))$ (ORD(t) lt CARD(t)) +
5      cash(t,l) + Liability(t,l);
```

Starting at line 1, the sum of incoming cash from sales of securities (less transactions costs), plus the holdings of cash from the previous stage (line 2), including interest, plus the premium of 100 mil. € received at stage T0 (line 3), must equal the total purchases (line 4), plus what is held in cash during the next stage, plus any payments of liabilities if these are included (line 5).

In the first model we use the simplest possible objective, maximizing the expected final wealth across scenarios. The latter is given as the difference between the cash accumulated and the discounted value (at stage T2) of the future payments, so we have:

```
WealthRatioDef(l)  ..
         wealth(l) =E= cash("t2",l) / FinalLiability(l);
```

```
ExpWealthObjDef ..
     z =E= SUM(l, wealth(l)) / CARD(l);
```

We introduce variables `wealth(l)` to collect, at the end of the horizon and under each scenario, the ratio between the cash available, `cash("t2",l)`, and the final liability `Final-Liability(l)`. The objective value, z, to be maximized is the average over all scenarios. At this point, all the constraints and variables of the model are indexed by scenario, but there is no connection among the scenarios

Logically, we need the model to return a single, unique solution to the investment problem, regardless of the scenario that may eventually be realized. To achieve this, we add non-anticipativity constraints to the model. These are constraints that force the first-stage decisions to be identical for all scenarios. Similarly, the second-stage decisions (at stage T1) must be the same for the UU and the UD scenario – because after the first stage, the

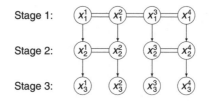

Figure 6.2: Illustration of the split-variable formulation corresponding to the scenario tree of Figure 6.1. Variables associated with each scenario/stage combination are shown. Horizontal double lines indicate non-anticipativity (equality) constraints among these variables.

model only sees that interest rates went up, not what they will do in the second stage – and for the DU and DD scenarios. The following constraints implement these non-anticipativity requirements:

```
NonAnticConOne(i,l)$(ORD(l) lt CARD(l)) ..
                hold("t0",i,l) =E= hold("t0",i,l+1);

NonAnticConTwo(i,l)$(ORD(l) eq 1 OR ORD(l) eq 3) ..
                hold("t1",i,l) =E= hold("t1",i,l+1);
```

This model indeed returns a solution that is implementable: At stage T0, invest 100M in PO7. If interest rates go up, then keep PO7 during the second stage; otherwise switch into IO2, which incurs a 1% loss due to transactions costs.

The formulation we have developed so far is characterized by a complete set of decision variables (buy, sell, hold) for each scenario, and additional non-anticipativity constraints that force the model not to be clairvoyant by using information that is not yet available when making first- and second-stage decisions. This formulation is known as a "split-variable" formulation – the (logically identical) first-stage variables are split up into one copy per scenario, and are then forced to be equal to each other with the additional constraints. In essence, the scenario tree of Figure 6.1 has been split up into the scenario structure shown in Figure 6.2. The decisions corresponding to each node have then been forced to agree, in accordance with the original scenario tree.

The ThreeStageSPDA.gms file contains several models that implement alternative objectives:

Model 1 implements the stochastic program with non-anticipativity constraints and no trans-action costs. The portfolio is not diversified since the objective function is to maximize expected return, and hence no risk measure is considered.

Model 2 implements the same as above but with transaction costs. Again, the initial invest-ment is not diversified, but the transaction costs reduce the rebalancing activity at stage T1.

Model 3 maximizes the worst-case outcome

$$\text{Max Min } W^l,$$

where W^l is the scenario-dependent final wealth. The Max-Min formulation is not a linear program. We create an equivalent linear program by adding a variable `WorstCase` that is defined to be less than or equal to each individual outcome, and then maximize it:

```
WorstCaseDef(l) ..    WorstCase =L= wealth(l);
```

```
SOLVE ThreeStageWorstCase MAXIMIZING WorstCase USING LP;
```

This model corresponds to extreme risk aversion and returns a diversified first-stage decision: 49.04% in `IO2` and 50.96% in `PO7`.

Model 4 maximizes the expected utility, using logarithmic utility. (See Definitions PFO-2.8.6 and PFO-2.8.7.)

```
UtilityObjDef ..    z =E= SUM(l, LOG (wealth(l) ) ) / CARD(l);
```

```
SOLVE ThreeStageUtility MAXIMIZING z USING NLP;
```

Here, the objective value is the expected logarithm of final wealth, and the model returns a solution with 98.1% in `IO2` and 1.9% in `PO7`.

Model 5 is a multi-stage formulation of the tracking Model PFO-5.3.4 with limits on maximum downside risk (see Section 5.3.1). In this case we constrain the final ratios to be greater than 1.1 – a constant benchmark – by allowing a tolerance `EpsTolerance` so that we have:

```
MADCon(l) ..    wealth(l) =G= 1.1 - EpsTolerance;
EpsTolerance = 0.09;
SOLVE ThreeStageMAD MAXIMIZING z USING LP;
```

The optimal portfolio is similar to that obtained by the worst case model (52.03% in `IO2` and 47.97% in `PO7`). In fact, both models strongly penalize deviation from a target, which, in the worst-case model, is endogenous.

In Figure 6.3 we summarize the optimal portfolios obtained by the four models. In Figures 6.4 and 6.5 we display the optimal dynamics of the `sell` and `buy` variables. Note that purchases occur only at stage `T0`, and thanks to the non-anticipativity constraints, the amount purchased is the same under all scenarios. Sales occurs at stage `T1`, to rebalance the portfolio, and at stage `T2`, to liquidate the portfolio and repay liabilities. For the selling variables, the non-anticipativity constraints are active at stage `T1`, and the optimal decisions are pairwise equal.

6.4.2   The FINLIB files

The GAMS source code and data for the models of this section are given in the following files:

- `ThreeStageSPDA.gms`

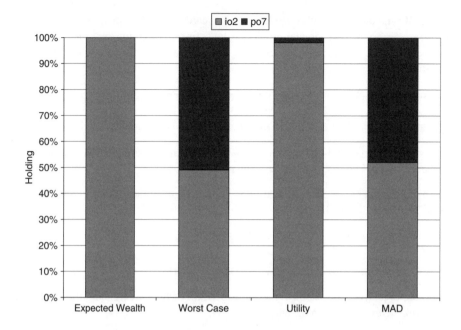

Figure 6.3: The optimal holdings for the three-stage SPDA model. The models with expected wealth as objective function do not diversify the investment. By introducing a risk measure, the investment is split between two assets.

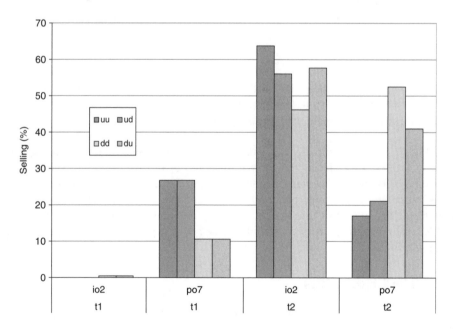

Figure 6.4: Sales under all scenarios and for each stage. Sales occur only at T1 and T2. Note that, the non-anticipativity constraints are active only at T1, and the optimal selling decisions are pairwise equal.

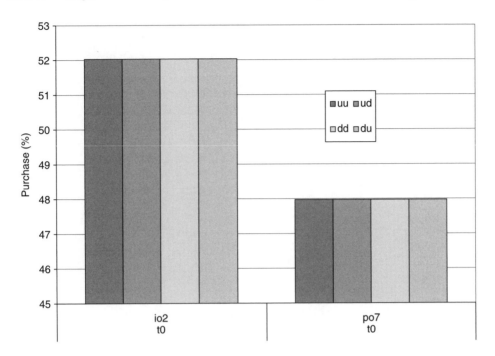

Figure 6.5: Purchases under all scenarios and for each stage. The non-anticipativity constraints equalize the optimal decision under each scenario. At T1 and T2, the purchases are zero.

Chapter 7

Index Funds

7.1 Preview

In this chapter we develop the GAMS models for structuring index funds. The development is based on the discussion of Chapters PFO-7 and PFO-10. The following models are discussed in this chapter and the GAMS source code for each is given in the associated FINLIB files:

Structural index funds implements a model for creating an index fund of fixed-income securities by matching two risk factors, duration and currency, based on Section PFO-7.3.1.

- `StructuralModel.gms`

Co-movement index funds implements a model for creating index funds by minimizing the tracking error between the portfolio return and the target index, based on Section PFO-7.3.2.

- `ComovementsModel.gms`

Selective hedging for index funds creates an indexation model that provides hedging for the exchange rate risk of an international portfolio, based on Section PFO-10.5.

- `SelectiveHedging.gms`

We implement and test the GAMS models of this chapter using two data sets stored in Excel files:

BondIndexData.xls contains 500 simulated returns of 254 bonds from three different countries, the United States, Germany, and Switzerland. It also contains scenarios of the USD/DEM and USD/CHF exchange rate, and of the return of the target index.

BroadIndexData.xls contains monthly return data for 10 asset classes over a 10-year period, including cash, stock and bond indices from the international markets. We also provide monthly data of the exchange rates covering the same period.

We use the utility GDXXRW to read the content of each file. The GAMS file Read-Data.gms in FINLIB performs the main task of reading data from the Excel files and delivering the manipulated data in GDX format. The file InputData.gdx will then be read for use by the model through the utility GDXIN.

7.2   Models for Index Funds

In this section we will customize some of the models described in Section 4.4 and Section 5.3 to deal with the specific task of building an index fund. We follow in our implementation the two approaches described in Section PFO-7.3. First, we adopt a structural approach, whereby indexed portfolios have to match some of the risk factors affecting the target index. The underlying idea is that if the portfolio and the index have the same key risk characteristics then they will have the same returns. In the co-movement approach we take next, the risk factors are not computed explicitly. Instead, we consider the index volatility as a measure of its risk factors, and the indexed portfolio is designed to be highly correlated with the target index. This is done by considering the correlations of the securities in the index and in the portfolio.

7.2.1   A structural model for index funds

A linear programming model for index funds based on the structural approach is given in Model PFO-7.3.1, and is reproduced here:

Model PFO-7.3.1 Linear program for index funds

$$\text{Maximize}\quad F(x) \tag{7.1}$$

$$\text{subject to}\quad \sum_{i=1}^{n} \delta_{ij} x_i = w_j, \qquad \text{for all } j \in \mathcal{K}, \tag{7.2}$$

$$\sum_{i=1}^{n} x_i = 1, \tag{7.3}$$

$$x \in X. \tag{7.4}$$

We implement this model using bonds from the three different countries in our data set. We structure the portfolio such that the percentages of bonds in each market are equal to those reported in the reference index. Furthermore, to mirror the risk factors of the target index in more detail we segment the duration of the securities in three classes as low, medium, and high, and then constrain the portfolio to hold in each duration class the same proportion of bonds as the reference index. The model could go on to segment the available securities by, say, market segment, credit rating class, and so on, and match the proportions in each class between the target index and the portfolio. Linear programming theory tells us that the more linear constraints we add the more non-zero variables we have in the optimal solution, and this implies more diversified portfolios. However, if we have as many risk factors as the securities in the index, thus capturing residual risk as well, we end up with a portfolio that is identical to the index – which is not very useful in practice.

We declare the set BxE (BB, EE), defined over the set of bonds (BB) and currencies (EE), to carry the partition of the bonds by currencies. The set BxD (BB, DD), defined over the set of bonds (BB) and duration levels (DD), carries the partition of the bonds by duration levels.

We define by `x(i)` the fraction of capital to be invested in each bond. The percentage holdings are defined by `CurrencyWeights(e)` and `DurationWeights(k)`.

```
PARAMETERS
   DurationWeights(k) / LOW 0.3, MEDIUM 0.2, HIGH 0.5 /
   CurrencyWeights(e) / USD 0.6, DEM 0.3, CHF 0.1 /;
```

Model PFO-7.3.3 Two-sided tracking model for index funds

$$\text{Maximize}_{x \in X} \quad \sum_{i=1}^{n} \bar{r}_i x_i \tag{7.5}$$

$$\text{subject to} \quad -\varepsilon \leq \sum_{i=1}^{n} r_i^l x_i - R_I(w, r^l) \leq \varepsilon, \qquad \text{for all } l \in \Omega, \tag{7.6}$$

$$\sum_{i=1}^{n} x_i = 1, \tag{7.7}$$

$$x \in X. \tag{7.8}$$

The currency and duration constraints are formulated by summing the variable `x(i)` over the sets `BxE` and `BxD`, respectively:

```
CurCons(e)..     SUM(i$BxE(i,e), x(i) ) =E= CurrencyWeights(e);

DurCons(k)..     SUM(i$BxD(i,k), x(i) ) =E= DurationWeights(k);
```

The rest of the equations are similar to those described in Section 4.4.

7.2.2   A co-movement model for index funds

The co-movement approach for index funds is similar to the tracking models developed in Section 5.3.1. However, the earlier models favor upside potential, and downside risk was limited by the user's risk appetite. In this section we are interested in replicating as close as possible the target index; hence, downside risk should be made as low as possible, which of course means that the upside potential is restricted as well. The two-sided tracking Model PFO-7.3.3 meets this requirement by limiting both upside and downside potential.

We use the same set of data as for the structural model. The two-sided tracking model is shaped through an additional constraint to limit the upside potential (see Model PFO-5.3.4 for comparison). The constraints on upside and downside are specified as follows:

```
TrackingConG(l)..    SUM(i, BondReturns(l,i) * x(i)) -
                     IndexReturns(l) =G= - EpsTolerance;

TrackingConL(l)..    SUM(i, BondReturns(l,i) * x(i)) -
                     IndexReturns(l) =L= EpsTolerance;
```

As seen in Section 5.3.1, the model is solved for decreasing values of the scalar `EpsTol-erance`. The minimum level of `EpsTolerance` for which Model PFO-7.3.3 is feasible determines the indexed portfolio. The indexed portfolios obtained with the two approaches are displayed in Figure 7.1.

7.2.3   A selective hedging model for index funds

Index funds that invest in foreign country assets are exposed to exchange rate risk between the asset currency and the investor's base currency. Currency risk can be hedged by entering in forward contracts, but this comes at a cost. In fact, a forward contract is nothing other than an insurance against unexpected changes in the value of the underlying asset.

With respect to hedging exchange rate risk, the portfolio manager can decide to fully hedge the portfolio, to leave currency risk unhedged, or to proceed with partial hedging whereby exchange rate exposure is partly covered by forward contracts. For example, a 50% hedge of the nominal amount invested in foreign countries means that only half of the total capital in foreign investments will be protected by futures. The hedging strategy whereby the hedge ratio is different for each currency included in the indexed portfolio is known as selective hedging. In selective hedging currency risk is hedged, perhaps only partially, for those currencies where data estimates dictate that currency movements are unfavorable, and remains unhedged for those currencies where the exchange rate changes appear favorable; see Chapter PFO-10 for a discussion of these issues.

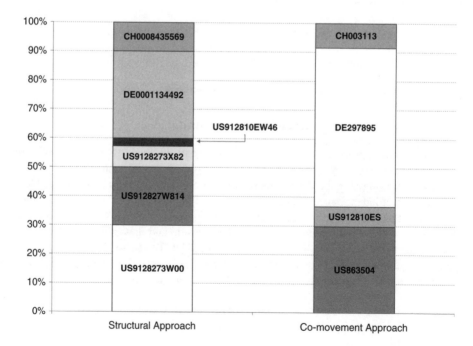

Figure 7.1: Indexed portfolios obtained from the structural and the co-movement approach. The two portfolios are designed to track an index of government bonds from three major countries.

The scenario optimization model for selective hedging is displayed in Model PFO-10.5.1 (see also Section PFO-7.3).

Model PFO-10.5.1 Scenario optimization for selective hedging

$$\text{Minimize} \quad \sum_{l \in \Omega} p^l \left| \sum_{i=1}^{n} \xi_i^l x_i - \left(\sum_{l \in \Omega} p^l \sum_{i=1}^{n} \xi_i^l x_i \right) \right| \tag{7.9}$$

$$\text{subject to} \quad \sum_{l \in \Omega} p^l \sum_{i=1}^{n} \xi_i^l x_i \geq \mu, \tag{7.10}$$

$$\sum_{i=1}^{n} x_i = 1, \tag{7.11}$$

$$x_i \geq 0, \qquad \text{for all } i \in U. \tag{7.12}$$

The model is implemented using data from `BroadIndexData.xls` for the broad market indices. The risk measure we adopt in building this model is that of MAD, but similar models can be built for CVaR, or expected regret minimization, or for expected utility maximization.

The key modeling concept in implementing a selective hedging model is to split the asset allocation variable `x(i)` in two parts: the unhedged position variable, `u(i)`, and the hedged position variable, `h(i)`.

Similarly, we define by `HedgedReturns(1,i)` and `UnhedgedReturns(1,i)`, respectively, the returns of the broad indices when exchange rate is hedged away through forward contracts, and the returns of the same indices when an unhedged position is taken. These are defined in GAMS as:

```
UnhedgedReturns(1,i)$(AxE(i,'EUR')) = AssetReturns(1,i,'EUR');

UnhedgedReturns(1,i)$(AxE(i,'USD')) = AssetReturns(1,i,'USD')
+ ExchangeRateReturns(1,'USD');

UnhedgedReturns(1,i)$(AxE(i,'JPY')) = AssetReturns(1,i,'JPY')
+ ExchangeRateReturns(1,'JPY');

UnhedgedReturns(1,i)$(AxE(i,'GBP')) = AssetReturns(1,i,'GBP')
+ ExchangeRateReturns(1,'GBP');;

HedgedReturns(1,i)$(AxE(i,'USD')) = AssetReturns(1,i,'USD')
+ EURUSDForwardRate;

HedgedReturns(1,i)$(AxE(i,'JPY')) = AssetReturns(1,i,'JPY')
+ EURJPYForwardRate;

HedgedReturns(1,i)$(AxE(i,'GBP')) = AssetReturns(1,i,'GBP')
+ EURGBPForwardRate;
```

Note that, for the domestic currency EUR, the exchange rate returns are zero under all scenarios.

The equations for the selective hedging model are obtained by simply substituting in place of `x(i)` the two new variables `u(i)` and `h(i)`. The return of the portfolio is now a function of the hedged and unhedged positions, and the MAD and return constraints become:

```
yPosDef(l) ..y(l) =G= SUM(i, UnhedgedReturns(l,i) * u(i)
                 + HedgedReturns(l,i) * h(i) ) -
                 SUM(s, pr(s) * SUM(i, UnhedgedReturns(s,i) * u(i)
                 + HedgedReturns(s,i) * h(i) ));

yNegDef(l) .. y(l) =G= SUM(s,pr(s)*SUM(i,UnhedgedReturns(s,i)*u(i)
                 + HedgedReturns(s,i) * h(i) )) -
                 SUM(i,  UnhedgedReturns(l,i) * u(i)
                 + HedgedReturns(l,i) * h(i) );

ReturnCon..      SUM(l, pr(l) * SUM(i, UnhedgedReturns(l,i) * u(i)
                 + HedgedReturns(l,i) * h(i))) =G= mu;
```

In Figure 7.2 we compare the efficient frontier obtained with the selective hedging model compared with the fully hedged and unhedged model. Note that the efficient frontier for

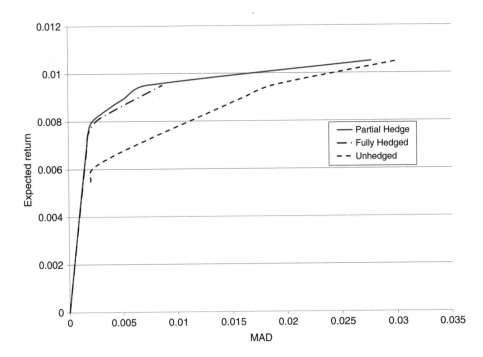

Figure 7.2: Efficient frontier of the selective hedging model vs the hedged and unhedged models. The selective hedging frontier dominates both the hedged and unhedged efficient frontiers.

selective hedging dominates both the fully hedged and unhedged efficient frontiers. This is as it should be, since selective hedging is the most general model, and it encompasses as special cases full hedging, no hedging and, with a small modification, partial hedging.

7.2.4   The FINLIB files

The GAMS source code and data for the models of this chapter are given in the following files:

- `StructuralModel.gms`

- `ComovementsModel.gms`

- `SelectiveHedging.gms`

- `BondIndexData.xls`

- `BroadIndexData.xls`

Chapter 8

Case Studies in Financial Optimization

8.1 Preview

In this chapter we develop the GAMS models for large-scale applications of portfolio optimization. The development is based on the discussion of Chapters PFO-10 to PFO-13. There are several important steps in going from an abstract description of the real-world problem, as described in PFO, to the implementable models we discuss here. These applications were developed by us and several collaborators over a number of years, and the models given in this chapter reflect various refinements that were developed in the implementation stage. These case studies can be used as the basis for the development of decision support systems to suit any special requirements.

The following models are discussed in this chapter and the GAMS source code for each is given in the associated FINLIB files:

International asset allocation provides models for investors that must track an international bond index while limiting their foreign exchange exposure. This model is based on Chapter PFO-10.

- BondIndex.gms

- BondIndexData.gms

Corporate bond portfolio management optimizes a portfolio of credit-risky assets following a passive, index fund, strategy. This model is based on Chapter PFO-11.

- Corporate.gms

- CorporateCVaR.gms

Minimum guarantee products develops models for the management of participating insurance policies with minimum guaranteed rate of return as discussed in Chapter PFO-12.

- GuaranteeModel.gms

Personal asset allocation provides a scenario optimization model for asset and liability management of individual investors, as described in Chapter PFO-13.

- PersonalAssetAllocation.gms

As seen in Chapter 2, GAMS can handle data having different formats. If, for example, data come from a provider and they are stored in Excel files, the GDXXRW utility is very handy for loading such data in the corresponding SETS and PARAMETERS. In general, a GDX container can also be used to store data obtained by some external programs, and then read in those data from the container itself.

However, writing directly from the simulator program to the GDX container is not always possible (we would need specific libraries to interface with). The simplest way to collect data from the simulator is to store them in plain ASCII or CSV format. In this way, GAMS can be also embedded in more complex systems where the optimization stage is only a part of the entire process.

Using GDX or ASCII files may imply a different setting of the data structures handled by GAMS. For this reason, we supply instances of the same case study when data are given in ASCII format or through a GDX container. The GDX containers are assembled starting from the plain ASCII files, so we also provide GAMS files to gather the plain data and then dump into a GDX container.

The FINLIB is also equipped with the following source files:

- GuaranteeModelData.gms

- GuaranteeModelGDX.gms

8.2   Application I: International Asset Allocation

A major Swiss bank manages several portfolios of government fixed-income securities, diversified internationally, using as a benchmark for their performance the World Government Salomon Brothers Index. Bank managers typically split the decision process into two steps: an asset allocation committee determines the exposure of the portfolio to each market, and then traders identify mispriced bonds in each market and construct the country-specific portfolio. The management is concerned with the relative lack of integration of these two functions. An optimization model could structure the decision making process, better integrate asset allocation with bond picking decisions and, perhaps, identify natural hedges among bonds in different currencies, thus resulting in improved portfolio performance.

In this section we describe the model developed to track a composite index of the international bond markets, thus providing support to the managers and traders of international portfolios. In order to cope with the volatility of the bonds and index return, we implement a mean absolute deviation MAD model over a set of scenarios of interest and exchange rates. Interest rate scenarios in multiple markets are used to estimate bond market changes in local returns, while the exchange rate scenarios convert returns to the local currency of Swiss francs. The model is based on the discussion in Section PFO-7.4 and in particular on Model PFO-7.4.4 that can incorporate operational and policy restrictions.

In Figure 8.1 we show the value of a 1,000 USD investment in a composite index from January 1, 1997 to July 1, 1998. This is the index we want to track. (For the purpose of this case study we do not use the Salomon Brothers global index, but a sub-index for managing a fund of investments in the US, Germany, and Switzerland.)

Scenarios of interest rates and exchange rates are generated according to the framework outlined in Section PFO-9.4.2. For each country we generate scenarios of the holding period returns of the bonds in the index and of the exchange rate against the base currency, in this

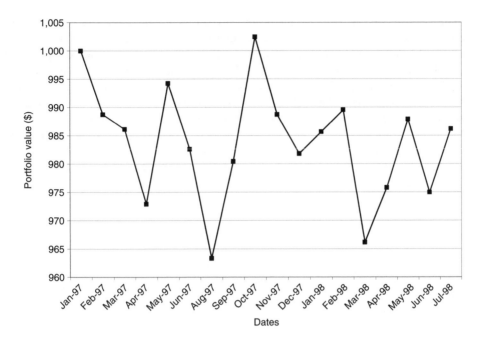

Figure 8.1: Value of a 1,000 USD investment in the composite index from January 1, 1997 to July 1, 1998.

case the Swiss franc (CHF). These scenarios are then combined to provide scenarios of the index. In particular, we calibrate our simulation model on a set of data obtained from the Salomon Brothers bond index for the United States, Germany, and Switzerland. The data are term structures and exchange rates from January 1990 to December 1996. Using the methodology of Section PFO-9.4.2 we estimate volatilities and correlations.

Model PFO-7.4.4 Operational model for index funds

$$\text{Maximize} \sum_{l \in \Omega} p^l R^l(x, y, z, v^+; r^l) \tag{8.1}$$

subject to $z_{ij} - x_{ij} + y_{ij} = b_{0ij}$,

$$\text{for all } i \in U, j \in \mathcal{K}, \tag{8.2}$$

$$\sum_{j=1}^{K} E_j^0 \left(\sum_{i=1}^{n} P_{0ij}^a x_{ij} \right) + v^+ - \sum_{j=1}^{K} E_j^0 \left(\sum_{i=1}^{n} P_{0ij}^b y_{ij} \right) = v_0 \tag{8.3}$$

$$-\varepsilon \leq R^l(x, y, z; r^l) - R_I(\gamma; r^l) \leq \varepsilon,$$

$$\text{for all } l \in \Omega, \tag{8.4}$$

$$x, y, z, v^+ \geq 0. \tag{8.5}$$

The model is run repeatedly for multiple dates. For instance, we first assume that the portfolio manager has to select a portfolio of bonds in January 1, 1997. Based on the term structure available on that date, and the historical volatilities and correlations from previous time periods, we calibrate the Monte Carlo simulation models, and generate scenarios of security and index returns. We then solve Model PFO-7.4.4 to select an indexed portfolio. The clock is then moved forward by one month and with the market data now available we can assess the performance of the portfolio. The model is run again using a new scenario set that applies to the new date. This process is repeated for each future date, using the latest information about the term structure and an updated correlation matrix.

The model is implemented in `BondIndex.gms` and it uses `BondIndexData.gdx` as its data. The GDX file is generated by `BondIndexData.gms` using the set of `.inc` files listed below. Note that some of these files contain the data generated by the simulation model. `BondIndexData.gms` contains the following set declarations and files:

```
SET Scenarios Scenarios set /SS_1 * SS_500/;

ALIAS(Scenarios,1,SS);

$OFFLISTING
$INCLUDE "BondsUniverse.inc"
$INCLUDE "BondPricesAccrualsUSD.inc"
$INCLUDE "BondPricesAccrualsDEM.inc"
$INCLUDE "BondPricesAccrualsCHF.inc"
$INCLUDE "InitialBondsAccruals.inc"
$INCLUDE "RiskFreeReinvestmentRates.inc"
$INCLUDE "Probabilities.inc"
$INCLUDE "IndexReturns.inc"
$INCLUDE "ExchangeRates-BondIndex.inc"
$ONLISTING

SETS
          Currencies Currencies set / USD US Dollar
                                       DEM German Mark
                                       CHF Swiss Franc  /

          Bonds       Bonds set    / #USDBND, #DEMBND, #CHFBND /;

ALIAS(Currencies,j);
ALIAS(Bonds,i);

SET
          JxI(j,i) Bonds by Currencies / USD.#USDBND, DEM.#DEMBND,
                                         CHF.#CHFBND /;
```

The file `BondsUniverse.inc` contains all the SETS that define the universe of available bonds by their CUSIP[1]. A sample of `BondsUniverse.inc` is reported here:

---

[1] CUSIP refers to both the Committee on Uniform Security Identification Procedures and the nine-character alphanumeric security identifiers that they (CUSIP) distribute for all North American securities.

```
SET USDBND      Bonds in the US market

        /USD_1   863048
        USD_2    863049

        ....

        ....
        USD_139          US912827ZN50
        USD_140          US912827ZX33/;
```

Note that we do not use the asset class CUSIP identifiers as labels, but use instead USD_1, USD_2, ..., USD_nn. This is because the CUSIP names given by data providers contain characters that are not allowed by GAMS (&, -, etc). Sometimes, the CUSIP is longer than 10 characters, which exceeds the GAMS limit for SET element names. With some patience it is possible to adjust these names to comply with the GAMS format. However, this is an error-prone and time-consuming procedure and the less meaningful but more mnemonic labels are used instead.

File BondPricesAccrualsXXX.inc stores bond prices (current and scenarios) and accruals, with XXX denoting the currency. The file also contains the parameter accounting for the outstanding values of each bond. Some of these bonds are callable, and under some scenarios they could be called. In these cases, the bond expires, and the outstanding value is set to zero; see the discussion on amortization factors in Section PFO-6.2.1. The cumulative risk-free interest rate, indexed by scenarios, is stored in file RiskFreeReinvestmentRates.inc, and file InitialBondsAccruals.inc stores the accrued interest for bonds held from the previous period: these data are used to determine the initial portfolio value in BondIndex.gms:

```
* Calculate initial portfolio value

HoldVal   = SUM(JxI(j,i), ExchangeRates0(j) * InitialHoldings(i)
                             * Price0(i));
InitAccrCash = SUM(JxI(j,i), ExchangeRates0(j) * InitialHoldings(i)
                             * Accruals0(i));
InitVal      = CashInfusion + InitAccrCash + HoldVal;
```

The remaining files store scenarios of index returns and exchange rates, and the probabilities associated with each scenario of interest rates and exchange rates for 500 realistic scenarios. These are sufficient to generate reasonably robust solutions, acceptable in the business setting.

8.2.1   Operational considerations

Usually, portfolio managers face a variety of operational and policy constraints. These are explicitly formulated in Model PFO-7.4.4. For example, the portfolio managers may not be allowed to trade more than 15 million CHF in Swiss bonds, since trades of this magnitude would create trading liquidity risk. Furthermore, to avoid concentration risk, the holdings in each instrument should not exceed 10 % of the total portfolio value. Once InitVal is computed, we use the UP and LO variable extensions to assign bounds on these operational requirements:

```
* Set the upper bound on the holdings

LOOP(JxI(j,i), Z0.UP(i) = InitVal/ExchangeRates0(j)/Price0(i)
    *UpprBnd );

* Set the limit on trading (sell or buy)
* CHF bonds for liquidity reasons

X0.UP(i)$JxI('CHF',i) = CHFtrade / Price0(i);
Y0.UP(i)$JxI('CHF',i) = CHFtrade / Price0(i);
```

Note that, the bounds on the holdings are in percentage of the portfolio value, which is expressed in USD. Hence, to determine the amount of face value in each currency, we need to transform the USD amount using the corresponding exchange rate.

The decision variables represent the amount of face values purchased or sold, and the holdings for each instrument available in each country. It is also possible to invest in cash, which is simply one more asset returning the risk-free rate. At the end of the holding period, the portfolio is liquidated at the final prices, and the terminal value is assigned to the scenario-dependent variable FinalCash(1):

The model constraints and the objective function implementation follow along the lines of Model PFO-7.4.4:

```
EQUATIONS

    ObjDef              Objective function definition (Expected return)
    CashInventoryCon    Cash balance equation today.
    FinalCashCon(1)     Cash balance equations at the end of first
                            stage.
    InventoryCon(i)     Constraints defining the asset inventory
                            balance
    MADCon(1)           MAD constraints;
```

The objective function measures the expected return of the tracking bond portfolio. Equation CashInventoryCon models the inventory of cash raised by selling bonds, the cash needed to buy bonds, and the amount of cash infused at the portfolio inception. Any remaining cash is accounted for by the variable Cash, which is invested at the risk-free rate for the next period:

```
ObjDef ..      z =E= 1000*SUM(1, pr(1)*(FinalCash(1)/InitVal - 1 ) );

CashInventoryCon ..    CashInfusion + SUM(JxI(j,i),
                       ExchangeRates0(j) * Y0(i) *
                       Price0(i) * (1-TrnCstS) )
                       =E= SUM(JxI(j,i),
                       ExchangeRates0(j) * X0(i) *
                       Price0(i)*(1+TrnCstB) ) + Cash;
```

The amount of face value sold and purchased has to balance out with the initial holdings and determines the holdings that will form the portfolio to be kept until the end of the horizon:

```
InventoryCon(i) .. InitialHoldings(i) + X0(i) =E= Y0(i) + Z0(i);
```

At the end of the horizon, the portfolio is liquidated (`FinalCashCon(l)`) and the value, under each scenario, is constrained to be as close as possible to the value of the target index, by putting a limit on the maximum deviation between the portfolio return and the index return (`MADCon(l)`):

```
FinalCashCon(l) ..  SUM(JxI(j,i),
                    ExchangeRates1(j,l) * Accruals1(i,l) * Z0(i))
                    + ReinvestmentRate(l) * Cash
                    + SUM(JxI(j,i),
                    ExchangeRates1(j,l) * Z0(i) * Outstanding(i,l) *
                    Price1(i,l) * (1-TrnCstS))
                    =E= FinalCash(l);


MADCon(l) ..   (FinalCash(l)/InitVal  - 1) - IndexReturns(l)
                    =G= - EpsTolerance;
```

The control parameter `EpsTolerance` determines the allowed tracking error of the portfolio return against the index return under each scenario. To determine the smallest possible value of tracking error `EpsTolerance` for which a feasible solution can be obtained, we set up a simple bisection algorithm that solves the model iteratively until the search interval is small enough. The extension `BondIndex.MODELSTAT` returns a value less or equal to 2 when a feasible solution is obtained, and it is used to guide the termination of the loop:

```
REPEAT
    EpsTolerance = (low+high)/2;
    SOLVE BondIndex USING LP MAXIMIZING z;
    IF(BondIndex.MODELSTAT <=2,
       high = EpsTolerance
    ELSE
       low  = EpsTolerance );
UNTIL (high-low) < 0.005 AND BondIndex.MODELSTAT <= 2;
```

8.2.2 Results

The model is now validated from different perspectives. First, we carry out an ex post analysis of the performance of the portfolios built using the model during the period January 1997 to July 1998. This analysis consists of selecting a tracking portfolio starting from January 1997, on the grounds of the simulation model calibrated on January 1997. We then move the clock a month forward (February 1997), at which point we know the precise index return, security returns, and exchange rates, and can thus determine the performance of our tracking portfolio and the tracking error. This completes one step of the backtesting. We then use the term structure of February 1997 to update the volatility and correlation estimates, recalibrate the Monte Carlo simulation models, and repeat the exercise. The process is repeated until July 1998, which is the last month for which we had data when this application was first developed. It is of course straightforward to extend the GAMS data sets to update the model with more recent data.

Using the Salomon Brothers G7 index we created a composite index consisting of equal holdings in two major currencies (USD and DEM) and the currency of the sponsoring institution (CHF). In Figure 8.2, we show the growth of 1,000 USD invested in the indexed portfolios, where the holdings in any particular bond must not exceed 5%, 10%, or 20% of the total portfolio value. We observe that the models perform well in tracking the volatile index.

The Sharpe ratios are 0.199 (when imposing the 5% bounds on the holdings in any single asset), 0.208 (for 10% bounds) and 0.202 (for 20% bounds). Note that these are ex post results so we do not necessarily expect the least constrained model to reach the best Sharpe ratio. We observe instead that the tightly constrained portfolio (with bounds of 5%) lags in performance compared to the less constrained portfolios, but beyond the 10% bound there is no performance improvement. In a sense, this performance should be expected as the bounds serve to reduce concentration risk, a form of risk that is not otherwise captured in the simulation data or other model constraints. In any case, the model performance is uniformly good if we consider that the Sharpe ratio of the index is -0.068.

We impose the additional constraint that no trades should exceed 15 million CHF, due to trading liquidity requirements in the Swiss market. We also keep the bound of 10% in the holdings of any single bond, and restrict the exposure to a single currency to remain within $\pm 15\%$ of weight of the particular currency in the index. This set of constraints reflects essentially all operational considerations of the portfolio managers. Results are shown in Figure 8.3, and the Sharpe ratio for the operational portfolios is 0.192, with a small drop to 0.189 when the net currency exposure is limited. This figure summarizes the most encouraging statistic about the model: It shows that it is possible to build indexed portfolios that satisfy operational requirements and perform well in tracking the composite index with out-of-sample data.

We benchmark the performance of the model by evaluating its performance against random portfolios. A valuable model should produce significantly better results compared to naive approaches – such as a randomly selected portfolio. We tested the performance of randomly selected portfolios of international government bonds over the period of our backtesting. The average monthly returns and standard deviation of returns over this period are shown in Figure 8.4 for 100 randomly selected portfolios. The same information is also reported for the Salomon Brothers index and for several portfolios constructed with our models. The optimized portfolios dominate consistently in the risk-return space. It is interesting though to note that only (approximately) one quarter of the randomly selected portfolios are dominated by the index. A manager who selects bonds by throwing darts at the bond pages is likely to perform well against the broad market index but not against competitors who use sophisticated models.

Finally, we test the efficacy of the integrated indexation model. To this end, we develop efficient frontiers using both the integrated and the nonintegrated models; see Section PFO-7.4. For the nonintegrated models, we first solve the asset allocation model and set the currency exposure to the one that yields the highest expected return. We then develop the efficient frontier of the portfolios in the three currencies such that the total exposure in each currency is equal to that determined by the asset allocation model. Figure 8.5 shows

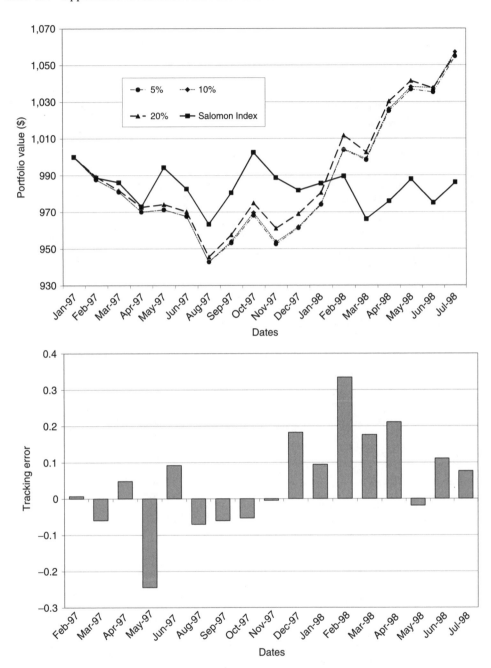

Figure 8.2: Value of a 1,000 USD investment in the composite index, and in indexed port-folios with bond holdings limited to 5%, 10%, and 20%, respectively, of the total portfolio value. (The figure at the bottom shows the monthly [annualized] tracking error of the portfolios with 20% limit on bond holdings.)

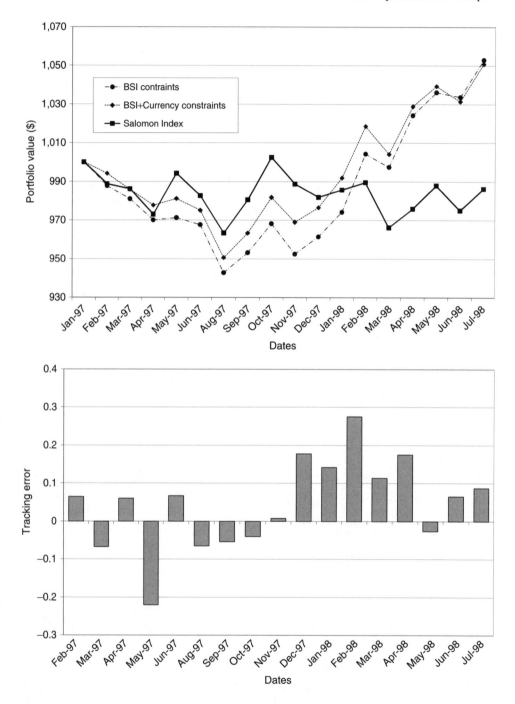

Figure 8.3: Value of a 1,000 USD investment in the composite index, and in indexed portfolios constrained by operational restrictions on liquidity (marked: BSI constraints) and
currency exposure (marked: BSI+currency constraints). (The figure at the bottom shows the
monthly [annualized] tracking error of the portfolios with liquidity and currency constraints.)

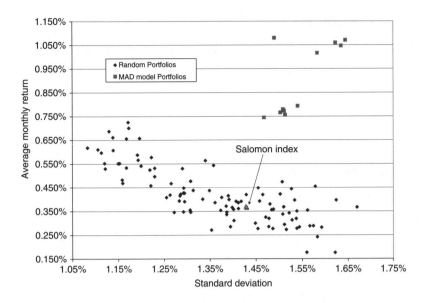

Figure 8.4: The risk-return profile of several model portfolios and 100 random portfolios during the testing period January 1997 to June 1998.

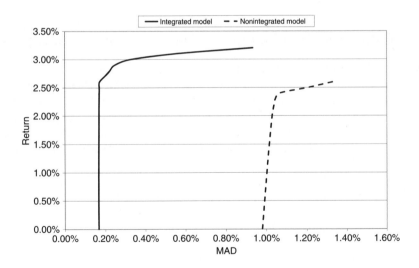

Figure 8.5: The positive effects of integrating several financial decisions in a common framework: the efficient frontier generated with the integrated model dominates the frontier generated using the nonintegrated models.

the efficient frontiers obtained with both the integrated and the nonintegrated models, and we note that the integration entails considerable benefits for the portfolio managers, by substantially reducing the volatility of the portfolio returns while also somewhat increasing the expected return.

8.2.3   The FINLIB files

The GAMS source code and data for the models of this section are given in the following files:

- `BondIndex.gms`

- `BondIndex.inc`

- `BondsUniverse.inc`

- `BondPricesAccrualsCHF.inc`

- `BondPricesAccrualsDEM.inc`

- `BondPricesAccrualsUSD.inc`

- `ExchangeRates-BondIndex.inc`

- `IndexReturns.inc`

- `InitialBondsAccruals.inc`

- `Probabilities.inc`

- `RiskFreeReinvestmentRates.inc`

8.3   Application II: Corporate Bond Portfolio Management

Corporate bond yields are heavily affected by default and migration risk. Their return distribution is usually very skewed and fat tailed. Using data generated by the model described in Chapter PFO-11, we implement here a model to select a portfolio to track a corporate bond index (see also Chapter PFO-7). The index is built artificially by simply weighting the returns of each available bond. We take into account the hierarchial decision process performed by fund managers, and, first, we solve the strategic decision among broad asset classes, as shown below:

Model PFO-11.5.1 Strategic model for corporate indexed funds

$$\operatorname*{Maximize}_{z \in X} \quad \sum_{l \in \Omega} p^l R(z, x; r^l) \tag{8.6}$$

$$\text{subject to} \quad -\epsilon \leq \sum_{j=1}^{K} R_j(w, r^l) z_j - R_I(\gamma, r^l) \leq \epsilon,$$

$$\text{for all } l \in \Omega, \tag{8.7}$$

$$\sum_{j=1}^{K} z_j = 1, \tag{8.8}$$

$$z \geq 0. \tag{8.9}$$

We then use the optimal broad asset allocation, z^*, to solve the tactical asset allocation model for bond picking, Model PFO-11.5.2 as reproduced here:

Model PFO-11.5.2 Tactical model for corporate indexed funds

For each $j \in \mathcal{K}$, solve :

$$\underset{x \in X}{\text{Maximize}} \quad \sum_{l \in \Omega} p^l R_{pj}(x; r^l) \tag{8.10}$$

$$\text{subject to} \quad - \epsilon \leq R_{pj}(x; r^l) - R_j(w, r^l) \leq \epsilon,$$

$$\text{for all } l \in \Omega, \tag{8.11}$$

$$\sum_{i=1}^{n} x_{ij} = \hat{z}_j, \tag{8.12}$$

$$x \in X. \tag{8.13}$$

The GAMS implementation starts with the construction of the index, and the broad asset classes used for the strategic asset allocation. Of course, for real cases, these are input parameters obtained from market data.

```
* Assign weights randomly

AssetWeights(i) = UNIFORM(1,10);

* Normalize the random weights

SCALAR
   WeightsSum;

WeightsSum = SUM(i, AssetWeights(i) );

AssetWeights(i) = AssetWeights(i) / WeightsSum;

* Compute broad asset weights in the index

BroadWeights('BA_1') =  SUM(m1, AssetWeights(m1) );
BroadWeights('BA_2') =  SUM(m2, AssetWeights(m2) );
BroadWeights('BA_3') =  SUM(m3, AssetWeights(m3) );

PARAMETER
   IndexReturns(l)        Index return scenarios
   BroadAssetReturns(j,l)    Broad asset class return scenarios
   Benchmark(l)           Current benchmark scenario returns;

* Build the broad asset classes
```

```
BroadAssetReturns('BA_1',1) =
    SUM(m1, AssetWeights(m1) * AssetReturns(m1,1));
BroadAssetReturns('BA_2',1) =
    SUM(m2, AssetWeights(m2) * AssetReturns(m2,1));
BroadAssetReturns('BA_3',1) =
    SUM(m3, AssetWeights(m3) * AssetReturns(m3,1));


* Build the index


IndexReturns(1) = SUM(j, BroadWeights(j) * BroadAssetReturns(j,1));
```

The structure of both models is very similar to that of general tracking models (see Section 5.3.1), and we briefly highlight here the main differences. In particular, we declare the definition of the portfolio return in two distinct ways to account for the strategic weights $z(j)$, and the tactical weights $x(i)$:

```
BroadPortRetDef(1).. PortRet(1) =E= SUM(j, z(j) *
                     BroadAssetReturns(j,1));


PortRetDef(1)..      PortRet(1) =E= SUM(a, x(a) *
                     AssetReturns(a,1));
```

The optimal weights obtained by solving the strategic model will serve as input for the tactical model: namely, the percentage invested in each bond must add up to Current-Weight:

```
BroadNormalCon..    SUM(j, z(j)) =E= 1.0;
NormalCon..         SUM(a, x(a)) =E= CurrentWeight;
```

Models PFO-11.5.1 and PFO-11.5.2 are, respectively, implemented as follows:

```
MODEL StrategicModel /ObjDef,BroadPortRetDef,MADCon,BroadNormalCon/;
MODEL TacticalModel /ObjDef,PortRetDef,MADCon,NormalCon/;
```

To solve the StrategicModel, we have to first set the index from which the deviations are computed. In particular we have that:

```
MADCon(1)..  PortRet(1) =G= Benchmark(1) - EpsTolerance;
```

For the StrategicModel, we select the optimal broad asset allocation such that deviations from the index, IndexReturns(1), are allowed within a tolerance EpsTolerance, so we have:

```
* Solve strategic model
Benchmark(1) = IndexReturns(1);
EpsTolerance = 0.02;


SOLVE StrategicModel USING LP MAXIMIZING ObjValue;
```

The `TacticalModel` is solved for each broad asset class, by setting `CurrentWeight` to the optimal value obtained from `StrategicModel`, and setting the index to be the current asset class. For example, for the broad asset class `BA_1`, we have that:

```
* Solve tactical model for Broad Asset 1 (BA_1)

CurrentWeight = z.L('BA_1');
Benchmark(l) = BroadAssetReturns('BA_1',l);
EpsTolerance = 0.02;
ACTIVE(i) = BroadAssetClassOne(i);
IF( CurrentWeight > 0.05,
    SOLVE TacticalModel USING LP MAXIMIZING ObjValue;
);
```

Note that we have used the same trick as in Section 3.5 to dynamically change the contents of `ACTIVE`. This allows us to set the domain of the securities belonging to each broad asset class.

The hierarchical decision process, and the models that follow, are shown to be sub-optimal (see Section PFO-7.4) compared to an integrated approach. The model that integrates the strategic and tactical asset allocation is given by `TacticalModel`, where we simply set:

```
CurrentWeight = 1.0;
Benchmark(l) = IndexReturns(l);
ACTIVE(i) = YES;
```

Finally, as stated in Section PFO-4.2, a correct risk measure is fundamental when dealing with corporate bonds. In particular, we need a measure that penalizes appropriately extreme events, when selecting the optimal portfolio. This is accomplished using a standard Conditional VaR model, and the corresponding GAMS model is contained in `Corporate-CVaR.gms`. We omit its description since it follows closely the implementation given in Section 5.5.

8.3.1   The FINLIB files

The GAMS source code and data for the models of this section are given in the following files:

- `Corporate.gms`

- `CorporateCVaR.gms`

- `CorporateCommonInclude.inc`

- `CorporateScenarios.inc`

8.4   Application III: Insurance Policies with Guarantees

The model we analyze in this section is a real-world application of optimal asset allocation for insurance products with guarantee. The model is discussed in Chapter PFO-12, and includes a complete analysis of the model, together with a discussion of empirical results. Model PFO-12.4.1 is repeated here; it has linear constraints and a nonlinear objective function:

Model PFO-12.4.1 Insurance policies with guarantees

$$
\underset{x \geq 0}{\text{Maximize}} \sum_{l \in \Omega} p^l U\left(\left\{(1+\rho) \prod_{t=1}^{T}(1+R_{pt}^l) + \right.\right.
$$

$$
+ \sum_{t=1}^{T}\left[y_{-t}^l - \Lambda_t^l(1+g+y_{+t}^l)\right]
$$

$$
\prod_{\tau=t+1}^{T}(1+R_{P\tau}^l)\prod_{\tau=1}^{t-1}(1+g+y_{+\tau}^l)(1-\Lambda_\tau^l) + \tag{8.14}
$$

$$
\left. - \prod_{t=1}^{T}(1-\Lambda_t^l)(1+g+y_{+t}^l)\right\}
$$

$$
\left. \left/\left[\rho\prod_{t=1}^{T}(1+r_{ft}^l) + \sum_{t=1}^{T}y_{-t}^l\phi(t,T)\prod_{\tau=1}^{t-1}(1-\Lambda_\tau^l)(1+g+y_{+\tau}^l)\right]\right)\right.
$$

s.t.
$$
\sum_{i \in \mathcal{U}} x_i = 1, \tag{8.15}
$$

$$
\beta R_{pt}^l - g = y_{+t}^l - y_{-t}^l, \quad \text{for } t = 1, 2, \ldots T, \text{ and for all } l \in \Omega, \tag{8.16}
$$

$$
R_{pt}^l = \sum_{i \in \mathcal{U}} x_i r_{ti}^l, \quad \text{for } t = 1, 2, \ldots T, \text{ and for all } l \in \Omega, \tag{8.17}
$$

$$
x \in X. \tag{8.18}
$$

For the empirical testing of the model, the asset classes considered are the indices of the Italian stock and bond markets, as displayed in Table 8.1. We generate scenarios of asset returns by bootstrapping a set of monthly records for the 10-year period from January 1990 to February 2000. Each scenario is a sample of returns of the assets obtained by sampling historical data. For each date in our sample, we read the returns of all assets during the month prior to that date, and this is one scenario of returns. Note that, with this approach, the correlations among asset classes are preserved. See Chapter PFO-9 for a discussion of scenario generation methods, and Section PFO-9.4.1 for the bootstrapping method used to generate the scenarios in this application.

In file `GuaranteeCommonInclude.inc` we declare the relevant SETS and SCALARS as follows:

```
SET TT Time span /TT_1 * TT_10/

SET SS Number of scenarios /SS_1 * SS_500/;

SET AA Set of Assets
```

Table 8.1: Stock and bond indices of the Italian market.

Code	Description
SBGVNIT.1-3	Salomon Brothers Italian Government Bond 1-3 years
SBGVNIT.3-7	Salomon Brothers Italian Government Bond 3-7 years
SBGVNIT.7-10	Salomon Brothers Italian Government Bond 7-10 years
ITMSBNK	Milan Mib Historic Banks
ITMSAUT	Milan Mib Historic Cars
ITMSCEM	Milan Mib Historic Chemicals
ITMSCST	Milan Mib Historic Construction
ITMSDST	Milan Mib Historic Distribution
ITMSELT	Milan Mib Historic Electronics
ITMSFIN	Milan Mib Historic Finance
ITMSFPA	Milan Mib Historic Finance Holdings
ITMSFMS	Milan Mib Historic Finance Misc
ITMSFNS	Milan Mib Historic Finance Services
ITMSFOD	Milan Mib Historic Food
ITMSIND	Milan Mib Historic Industrials
ITMSINM	Milan Mib Historic Industrials Misc
ITMSINS	Milan Mib Historic Insurance
ITMSPUB	Milan Mib Historic Media
ITMSMAM	Milan Mib Historic MineralsMetals
ITMSPAP	Milan Mib Historic Paper
ITMSMAC	Milan Mib Historic Plants & Machine
ITMSPSU	Milan Mib Historic Pub Util Serv
ITMSRES	Milan Mib Historic Real Estate
ITMSSER	Milan Mib Historic Services
ITMSTEX	Milan Mib Historic TextileClothing
ITMST&T	Milan Mib Historic Trans & Tourism

```
   /AA_1          SBGVNIT.1-3
    AA_2          SBGVNIT.3-7
    AA_3          SBGVNIT.7-10
    ....          .....
    AA_25         ITMSTEX
    AA_26         ITMST&T/;
```

The meaning of the three SETS is self-explanatory. With the SCALARS statement below, we input the parameters that will be used by the optimization model and in the post-processing phase:

```
SCALARS
    mig      Minimum Guarantee /0.04/
    ptr      Participation Rate /0.85/
    ili      Initial Liability /1.0/
    txr      Tax Rate for Shareholders /0.51/
    rho      Equity Ratio /0.04/;
```

```
ALIAS(SS,1);
ALIAS(TT,t,k);
ALIAS(AA,i,j);
```

The scenarios of asset returns, which are bootstrapped from the set of historical data, are stored in AssetReturns-Guarantee.inc. The parameter ar(1,t,i) has three indices to take into account the dependence of asset returns on the asset class set (i), the time set (t), and the scenarios set (1). The file PeriodicCapFactors.inc and CapFactors.inc store, respectively, the risk-free capitalization factor, rolled from period t to the end of the horizon T, $\phi^l(t, T)$, and the risk-free capitalization factor over the entire horizon, $\phi^l(0, T)$. Both parameters are scenario dependent and they are input to GAMS as a TABLE (respectively, they are pcf(1,t) and cf(1)).

Finally, the file AbandonProbabilities.inc contains the probability of abandoning the policy. The probability that a policyholder abandons the policy is Probability(death) + Probability(lapse). In the GAMS model, we set the lapse probabilities to zero and use probabilities of death from the Italian mortality tables.

The next fragment of code contains the VARIABLES declarations. Note that HO(i) corresponds to the asset holdings x_i; YP(1,t) and YM(1,t) correspond, respectively, to y^l_{+t} and y^l_{-t}:

```
POSITIVE VARIABLES
    HO(i)       Asset holdings.
    YP(1,t)     yPlus - surplus in excess of  minimum guarantee.
    YM(1,t)     yMinus - deficit in lack of minimum guarantee.;
```

We now turn to the equations that define the nonlinear programming model. The most complicated expression is the objective function (8.14). We assume a logarithmic utility function corresponding to growth-optimal policies:

To improve readability of the coding, we split OFe in three parts that represent, respectively, Equations PFO-12.27, PFO-12.17, and PFO-12.21:

```
* Final asset value
((1+rho) * PROD (t, (1+PRT(1,t))) + SUM(t, ((YM(1,t) -
(abp(t) * (1.0 + mig + YP(1,t)))) * PROD(k$(ORD(k) >
ORD(t)), (1.0 + PRT(1,k))) * PROD(k$(ORD(k) <
ORD(t)), ((1 - abp(k)) * (1.0 + mig + YP(1,k))))))
```

```
* Final liability value
PROD(t,((1 - abp(t)) * (1.0 + mig + YP(1,t)))))
```

```
* Final equity value (( rho * cf(1)) + SUM(t, YM(1,t) * pcf(1,t) *
PROD(k$(ORD(k) < ORD(t)), (1 - abp(k)) * (1.0 + mig +
YP(1,k))))))
```

Note how the $-operator is used to control the domain of operation of the PROD operator to model the $\prod_{\tau=t+1}^{T}$ factor in Equation PFO-12.27. Since the PROD operator is executed over a t subset, we declare an alias set k and condition the operation PROD using k. For example, to implement the product operator $\prod_{\tau=t+1}^{T}$ we condition k to start from ORD(t)+1, thus ignoring all previous time indices. This is obtained by forcing the index k with the dollar condition k$(ORD(k)>ORD(t)). The product operator $\prod_{\tau=1}^{t-1}$ is displayed in the following code segment:

```
PROD(k$(ORD(k) < ORD(t),..).
```

Here the $-operator filters out all indices k greater than the current (ORD(t) - 1).

Constraints (8.15), (8.16) and (8.17) of the model are straightforward to implement and they are given in the following code segment:

```
BAe..    SUM(i, HO(i)) =E= 1.0;


PRTd(l,t)..    PRT(l,t) =E= SUM(i, (HO(i) * ar(l,t,i)));


YPMSd(l,t)..    (ptr * PRT(l,t) - mig) =E= YP(l,t) - YM(l,t);
```

When solving difficult nonlinear models it is a good practice to narrow the solution space and provide a good starting point. To assist the solver in finding a feasible solution, we set the level attribute (.L) of the variables to an initial value, and impose bounds on some of the variables.

```
* Guess an initial solution and set bounds on variables
HO.UP(i) = 1.0;

HO.L(i) = 0.0;
HO.L('i_1') = 0.8;
HO.L('i_2') = 0.2;

PRT.L(l,t) = SUM(i, (HO.L(i) * ar(l,t,i)));
YM.L(l,t) = - MIN ((ptr * PRT.L(l,t) - mig), 0);
YP.L(l,t) = MAX ((ptr * PRT.L(l,t) - mig), 0);
```

In the post-optimization phase, we determine the cost of the guarantee and the net annualized after-tax certainty equivalent excess return on equity; see, respectively, Equations PFO-12.14 and PFO-12.47.

```
* Post-Optimization Calculation and Output

SCALARS

   OptimalCeXRoe     Optimal certainty equivalent excess Return-On-
                        Equity
   AnnualNetCeXRoe   Annual equivalent, net of tax, of the Optimal
                        CeXRoe
   ExpGuarCost       Expected guarantee cost;


PARAMETERS


FinalEquity(l)    Final equity level;
OptimalCeXRoe = EXP ( EUROE.L );
```

```
FinalEquity(l) = ( rho * cf(l) ) +
               SUM(t, YM.L(l,t) * pcf(l,t) *
               PROD( k$(ORD(k) < ORD(t)),
               ((1 - abp(k)) * (1.0 + mig + YP.L(l,k))))));

ExpGuarCost = (1.0 / CARD(l) ) * SUM (l, (FinalEquity(l) / cf(l))
               - (rho * ili) );

AnnualNetCeXRoe = ((OptimalCeXRoe)**(1/CARD(t)) - 1) * (1 - txr);
```

A complete analysis of the model, together with a discussion of empirical results, are given in Chapter PFO-12.

8.4.1   The FINLIB files

The GAMS source code and data for the models of this section are given in the following files:

- `GuaranteeModel.gms`

- `GuaranteeCommonInclude.inc`

- `AssetReturns-Guarantee.inc`

- `CapFactors.inc`

- `PeriodicCapFactors.inc`

- `AbandonProbabilities.inc`

8.5   Application IV: Personal Financial Planning

In this section we develop a scenario optimization model for asset and liability management of individual investors based on the application discussed in Chapter PFO-13, where a

Table 8.2: Benchmarks and corresponding asset classes.

Code	Description
MSNAMR	Stocks North America
MSPACF	Stocks Pacific
MSEMKG	Stocks Emerging Countries
MSEMUI	Stocks EMU
MSEXEM	Stocks Ex-EMU
JPMUSU	Bonds North America
JPMJPU	Bonds Pacific
JAGALL	Bonds EMU
JPMUKU + SBSZEUE	Bonds Ex-EMU
JPMPTOT	Bonds Emerging Countries
JPEC3M	Cash

comprehensive analysis of the model is given together with a discussion of results obtained using a web-based system implementing the model. We consider, in particular, the optimization of the portfolio of an individual investor, who has a given level of initial wealth and wishes to reach a target goal within some time horizon. The individual must determine an asset allocation strategy so that the portfolio growth rate will be sufficient to reach the target. The model is given in PFO-Model 13.5.1 and is repeated here:

Model PFO-13.5.1 Personal financial planning

$$\text{Maximize} \quad \sum_{l \in \Omega} p^l \sum_{t=1}^{T} y_{+t}^l \Phi^l(t, T) \tag{8.19}$$

subject to

$$\sum_{l \in \Omega} p^l \sum_{t=1}^{T} y_{-t}^l \Phi^l(t, T) \leq \omega \tag{8.20}$$

$$\sum_{i=1}^{n} x_i = 1 \tag{8.21}$$

$$R_{pt}^l = \sum_{i=1}^{n} x_i r_{it}^l, \text{ for } t = 1, 2, \ldots T, l \in \Omega, \tag{8.22}$$

$$R_{pt}^l - g_t^l = y_{+t}^l - y_{-t}^l, \text{ for } t = 1, 2, \ldots T, l \in \Omega. \tag{8.23}$$

The set of asset classes is represented by various market benchmark indices as summarized in Table 8.2. Scenarios are generated by bootstrapping a set of historical monthly records for the 13-year period from January 1988 to February 2001. To take into account the different currencies, we considered the historical monthly records of the exchange rates for the currency of each asset class to the base currency, and proceeded to sample them in conjunction with the returns of the selected benchmarks. Each scenario is a vector of returns of the assets obtained by sampling returns that were observed during this period.

The GAMS model is run with a fixed planning horizon (nbryears), target growth rate (grr), and risk tolerance (lambda). These data are stored in PersonalCommon-Include.inc:

```
SET TT Time span /TT_1 * TT_10/

SET SS Set of scenarios /SS_1 * SS_1000/;

SET AA Set of Assets
    /AA_1    MSNAMR
     AA_2    MSPACF
     ...     ...
     AA_13   JPUS3M
     AA_14   JPJP3ML/;
```

```
SCALARS
    grr          Growth rate /0.04/
    agrr         Annual growth rate /0.04/
    lambda       Risk Aversion /1.1/
    omega        Risk Level /0.1/
    nbryears     Number Of Years /10/
    ipv          Initial portfolio value /1/;
```

```
ALIAS(SS,l);
ALIAS(TT,t,k);
ALIAS(AA,i,j);
```

The time horizon is split in 10 time steps (t), and we test the model using 1000 scenarios (l). Given a growth rate `grr` and scenarios of the inflation rate, the quantity $\Phi^l(t, T)$ (see Definition PFO-13.28) can be computed a priori. The file `LiabilityScenarios.inc` contains data for the parameter `lblty(l,t)`, accounting for the product $\prod_{\tau=0}^{t-1}(1 + g_\tau^l)$; the file `CapFactorsScenarios.inc` contains data for the parameter `cfs(l,t)`, accounting for the product $\prod_{\tau=t}^{T}(1 + r_{f\tau}^l)$. Finally, the scenarios of price appreciation can be found in `InflationScenarios.inc`, and are handled through the parameter `infltn(l,t)`.

All these files are written in comma-separated format (CSV), and the input is carried out through the INCLUDE statement, with the dollar control option ONDELIM/OFFDELIM to handle the comma delimiter:

```
PARAMETER ar(l,t,i)
/
$ONDELIM
$INCLUDE "AssetReturns.inc";
$OFFDELIM/;
PARAMETER lblty(l,t)
/
$ONDELIM
$INCLUDE "LiabilityScenarios.inc";
$OFFDELIM
/;
PARAMETER infltn(l,t)
/
$ONDELIM
$INCLUDE "InflationScenarios.inc"
$OFFDELIM
/;
PARAMETER cfs(l,t)
/
$ONDELIM
$INCLUDE "CapFactorsScenarios.inc"
$OFFDELIM
/;
```

The model for personal asset allocation uses elements of the model developed for insurance products with guarantee (see Section 8.4) and the put/call models (see Section 5.7). The variables of the problem are:

```
POSITIVE VARIABLES
   HO(i)             Asset holdings
   YP(l,t)           yPlus - surplus in excess of growth rate.
   YM(l,t)           yMinus - deficit in lack of growth rate.;
```

The variables `YP(l,t)` and `YM(l,t)` have the same meaning as variables y_+^l and y_-^l in Models PFO-5.7.1 and PFO-12.4.1. They are defined through the following equation:

```
YPMd(l,t)..  SUM( i, (HO(i) * ar(l,t,i))) - (grr +
                 infltn(l,t)) =E= YP(l,t) - YM(l,t);
```

The reward measure to be maximized is the expected value of the upside deviations from the growth rate `grr`; the risk measure we wish to limit is the expected value of the downside deviations from the same growth rate. Coded in GAMS they are given by:

```
OFe..   OF =E= (1.0/CARD(l)) * SUM(l, SUM(t, lblty(l,t) *
         YP(l,t) * cfs(l,t)));
PUTe .. SUM(l, SUM(t,lblty(l,t) * YM(l,t) * cfs(l,t))) /
         CARD(l)  =L= omega;
```

Recall that this formulation will deliver a solution with both `YP(l,t)` and `YM(l,t)` non-zero when `omega` is not small enough to make `PUTe` an active constraint; see the discussion in Section 6.2.1.

When building an efficient frontier, we can control this event through the marginal value of the `PUTe` equation. In fact, when the constraint is inactive, the marginal value is zero, whereas if it is active the marginal value is greater than one.

An alternative formulation of Model PFO-13.5.1 is to use an objective function that maximizes the expected upside and minimizes the expected downside, by penalizing the latter by a weight `lambda` strictly greater than one as follows:

```
OFPCe.. OF =E= (1.0/CARD(l)) * (SUM(l, SUM(t, lblty(l,t)*
         YP(l,t) * cfs(l,t))) - lambda *
         SUM(l, SUM(t,lblty(l,t) * YM(l,t) * cfs(l,t))));
```

We solve both models on the same set of data. Note that, either `omega` or `lambda` is set such that both `YP(l,t)` and `YM(l,t)` are non-zero (it suffices that `lambda` is strictly greater than one). This can be checked by displaying the parameter `YpYm(l,t)`, which contains the products of the optimal `YP.L(l,t)` and `YM.L(l,t)`.

```
*  Model that maximizes the Call side with  bound on the Put side
MODEL PersonalModelOne /OFe,PUTe,BAe,YPMd/;

SOLVE PersonalModelOne USING LP MAXIMIZING OF;

*  Model that maximizes the Call side and minimizes the Put side
```

```
MODEL PersonalModelTwo /OFPCe,BAe,YPMd/;

SOLVE PersonalModeltwo USING LP MAXIMIZING OF;

PARAMETER
   YpYm(l,t);

YpYm(l,t) = YP.L(l,t) * YM.L(l,t);

DISPLAY YpYm
```

8.5.1   The FINLIB files

The GAMS source code and data for the models of this section are given in the following files:

- `PersonalAssetAllocation.gms`

- `PersonalCommonInclude.inc`

- `AssetReturns-PersonalAssetAllocation.inc`

- `LiabilityScenarios.inc`

- `InflationScenarios.inc`

- `CapFactorsScenarios.inc`

Bibliography

[1] A. Brooke, D. Kendrick, and A. Meeraus. *GAMS: A User's Guide, Release 2.25*. The Scientific Press, Boyd and Fraser Publishing Company, Danvers, US, 1992.

[2] Y. Censor and S.A. Zenios. *Parallel Optimization: Theory, Algorithms, and Applications*. Numerical Mathematics and Scientific Computation. Oxford University Press, New York, 1997.

[3] H. Dahl. A flexible approach to interest rate risk management. In S.A. Zenios, editor, *Financial Optimization*, chapter 8, pages 189–208. Cambridge University Press, Cambridge, UK, 1993.

[4] S.G. Nash and A. Sofer. *Linear and Nonlinear Programming*. McGraw-Hill, New York, 1996.

[5] S. Uryasev and R.T. Rockafellar. Optimization of conditional value–at–risk. *Journal of Risk*, **2**(3),21–41, 2000.

[6] S.A. Zenios. *Practical Financial Optimization: Decision Making for Financial Engineering*. Blackwell Publishing, Cambridge, MA, 2007.

Index

Figures and Tables are indicated by *italic page numbers*, footnotes by suffix 'n'

Index compiled by Paul Nash